ALL ABOARD

A School Board Gets on Track

by

Charles Tollett, EdD

and

Dan Tollett, EdD

Outskirts Press, Inc.
http://www.outskirtspress.com

Paperback ISBN: 978-1-9772-3191-8
Hardback ISBN: 978-1-9772-3467-4

Library of Congress Control Number: 2020917175

PRINTED IN THE UNITED STATES OF AMERICA

Table of Contents

Foreword

by Dr. Mark Edwards and Dr. Terry Grier

School Board decisions have a huge impact on millions of children and their families, as well as most communities in America. How do individual School Board members become an effective School Board? We would advocate as the authors do, that embracing learning as both individuals and as an elected body is an absolute key. The complexity and variation of issues that School Boards face today require leaders who are committed to learning, growing and serving children.

Drs. Dan and Charles Tollett provide an excellent compilation of the policies and practices of an evolving school board through the lens of Progress County School Board and its members. The real-world discussions reveal to the reader a view of policy and vision work by school board members and how they grapple with finding common ground. By presenting an array of the myriad challenges of today's schools and how the individual board members learn to work together, while respecting differences, is of particular importance. Valuable insight into the importance of discussion, debate, listening and problem solving as a collective body, while dealing with different personalities and backgrounds is of huge importance. School Boards that work well together have greater success than those that don't.

The authors (both with immense experience working with school boards) offer school board members real time examples of everything from budgets to the pandemic and how the Progress County School Board handles them. How to work with the Superintendent and build a positive working relationship through this lens will resonate and be of value. More than ever before, communities are in need of leadership for their school systems and students. "All Aboard" can serve as an excellent resource for school boards to use as a framework for improvement and success. It provides clear guidance to answering the all-important question that should be on the minds of all school boards, "What does the board need to do to make sure ALL students graduate from high school with the skills needed to be successful in tomorrow's world?"

Dr. Mark Edwards is the retired Superintendent, Mooresville, North Carolina. He was the 2013 national superintendent of the year. He served as Dean of the University of North Alabama School of Education and Superintended of Henrico County and Danville school systems in Virginia.

Dr. Terry Grier served as a school superintendent for 32 years, leading rural, suburban, and urban school districts. Eighty-six of the women and men with whom he worked have gone on to become superintendents across America. Dr. Grier was named North Carolina and Texas Superintendent of the Year; The National Educator of the Year by The Council of Great City Schools; and, AASA's Effie Jones Award for his support of women and minorities in Education. He led the Houston Independent School District to become the first district in the country to win the prestigious Broad Prize in Education for a second time.

Preface

Is there a more challenging elective position than being a member of a local school board? School board members are not off in Washington or in the state capital away from the everyday scrutiny of their constituents. No, they do their work making decisions as they govern public schools right in the community where their constituents live. And, their decisions affect the thing Americans care most about, their children.

Congressmen and state legislators go away to the state or national capital to do their work and, to a large extent, they tell their constituents what they want them to know and frequently they are able to disguise their unpopular votes. Not so with local school board members. Citizens attend their meetings when they are concerned about a decision that's upcoming. And, whether they are well informed about an issue or not, some are more than willing to offer their opinions about how school board members should vote. They do not seem reluctant to share their criticism when they don't like the vote of a local school board member.

Far too many citizens consider themselves to be experts in matters regarding public education because about everyone in the community either attended public schools or they know someone who did. Seldom does an issue arise that has the support of the entire community. There usually seems to be a significant number of people who are adamant in their support of an issue and an equal number who oppose. It's no great surprise that each group seems to be able to find a champion for their cause who has influenced at least one member of the school board.

Issues that the Progress County Board deals with are issues that most boards face. This book is not designed to tell school board members how they should vote on issues. Rather, it provides school board members with the opportunity to consider opposing positions presented by others without the pressure of making decisions themselves. Although members of the Progress County board disagree and occasionally behave in a manner unbecoming of school board members, the board, as a whole, provides examples of how a school board might come together even when members strongly disagree.

It raises the issue of school board leadership. What is the school board's role in determining what a school district should become? Should a school board lead? Or, is the school board simply a problem solving body? Should a school board initiate change or are school boards relegated to reacting to proposals by school administrators? The Progress County School Board wrestles with these questions and explores the issue of establishing goals and leading in a single direction.

Is it possible for an elected school board to disagree agreeably? The Progress County Board explores the question of what it wants to be and how it can be effective. As it considers a number of issues it also weighs how the process of making those decisions might help their school board come together to be a better board.

At the end of each chapter, one board member, Mark, reflects on the decisions of the board and shares his reflections with the reader. The tone of the book departs from the dualistic thinking that asks **what should we do?** and encourages consideration of the question *in what ways might we think and act to accomplish our purpose?*

Uses of this Book

All Aboard is the story of the Progress County Board of Education getting on track and becoming an effective school board in spite of deep philosophical differences among its members. It's about a school board, however, the principles apply to other boards as well. This book lends itself to being read by individual board members, CEOs, superintendents, or citizens who would like to better understand how boards effectively function.

A person considering candidacy for a board can add greatly to qualification for board service by reading **All Aboard** before making public statements to support his/her interest.

Other uses of the book include board retreats, workshops and academies for board members, sessions at conventions and board development activities conducted by associations, as well as college and university courses for administrators who must know how to work effectively with a board.

In short, persons interested in board development or working effectively with a board will find themselves better prepared by reading, reflecting upon and discussing the experiences of this fictional board.

About the Authors

The authors are brothers, the two youngest of a family of eleven children, nine boys and two girls. They grew up on a small farm in the mountains of Tennessee. Their father was a farmer and their mother was a teacher and one of the first female school superintendents in Tennessee.

Charles Tollett was a superintendent of schools in several districts after teaching and coaching at elementary and secondary levels in his home county. While serving as Superintendent of his home county, he was elected Chairman of the Board for LBJ&C Development Corporation- a multi-county community action agency during the "War on Poverty." In Cleveland, TN, he served in three positions: Director of the Southeast Tennessee Educational Cooperative, Assistant Superintendent of Cleveland City Schools, and Dean of the College at Cleveland State Community College.

Charles was Executive Director of the Tennessee School Boards Association at a time when the position was a joint one with the University of Tennessee. He accepted the opportunity to teach education in an adjunct capacity at UT Nashville, Tennessee Technological University, and Lee University. After serving at TSBA, he became Assistant Commissioner for Research and Development in the Tennessee Department of Education. He retired from the Superintendency of Kingsport City Schools to become a Senior Program

Associate at the Center for Creative Leadership in Greensboro, North Carolina, where he focused on working with school boards, superintendents, and other school administrators.

After completing elementary and secondary school in Cumberland County, TN. he earned a Bachelor's degree in biology from Carson-Newman College (now CNU), a Master of Science degree in Mathematics from the University of Mississippi, a Master of Arts degree from George Peabody College (now of Vanderbilt University), and a Doctorate in Educational Administration and Supervision from the University of Tennessee. His dissertation was "A Study of the Tennessee School Boards Association - Its Functions and Effectiveness as Perceived by Board Members and Superintendents."

After full retirement he returned to his hometown, where he was elected to the Cumberland County School Board and was chosen chairman of that board. In every community where he lived he was involved and active with the school board in whatever capacity that was available. In at least three communities he assisted with the Leadership Development Program of the Chamber of Commerce. Charles has frequently served as a presenter at state and national school board conventions and meetings of those of a wide variety of other interests.

Dan Tollett retired after serving as Executive Director of the Tennessee School Boards Association for twenty five years. He was Chairman of the Department of Educational Administration, Supervision and Curriculum at Tennessee Technological University for eight years and later taught instructional leadership in the Department of Secondary Education at the University of North Alabama. He has taught every grade from fourth grade through graduate school. He's also been a school principal, coach and central office staff member and a program director at the Oak Ridge Educational Cooperative.

As a professor, he frequently worked with local school boards and on multiple occasions was a speaker at the National School Boards Annual Convention. As Executive Director of the Tennessee School Boards Association, he conducted seminars and workshops for school boards in thirty-three states and has been a frequent presenter at National School Boards Association Annual Conventions.

He was elected as Chairman of the State Association Executive Directors NSBA Liaison Committee in 1998 and, in that position, served as an ex officio member of the Board of Directors of the National School Boards Association.

He was the founder and current Administrator of Utrust, an organization that assists school boards in Tennessee with employment and unemployment issues. It sponsors the Utrust Appreciation Program which seeks, through student leadership, to recognize and express appreciation to school employees and in turn promotes recognition and appreciation of students by school staff. Utrust has recently made mini-grants of more than $5 million to Tennessee schools for things teachers need to teach more effectively.

He earned a Bachelor's Degree in Mathematics from Middle Tennessee State University, a Masters Degree in Educational Administration and Supervision from Tennessee Technological University and a Doctorate in Educational Administration and Supervision from the University of Tennessee.

Both authors have written numerous school board development materials and have written extensively about school boards in articles for state school boards association publications as well as the American School Board Journal.

CHAPTER 1

How It All Started

"WHAT HAVE I gotten myself into?" asked Mark as he looked in the mirror. "I sure hope this is what I want to do. Well, ready or not, here I come."

With that, Mark Trent launched the day of his first official responsibility as a school board member in Progress County. He was one of three newly elected members of the seven-member board. Friends and neighbors had urged him to run for the seat because they were not pleased with the way the schools were being run. There was a general feeling in the community that the board, as presently constituted, was merely maintaining the status quo. Many citizens thought that the board was doing little or nothing to advance the quality of the community's schools. Clearly, the community did not hold the board in high esteem.

Friends thought Mark would be able to influence other members to look at things in a different way. He was not one to be satisfied with the status quo; rather, he was consistently seeking a better way to do whatever he did. He also had a knack for helping make complicated issues understandable and solutions to difficult problems seem achievable. Although he was highly intelligent and a clearly a visionary, most people did not feel threatened by him or uneasy in discussions with him.

Mark had grown up in the community and had gone on to be a teacher and ultimately Superintendent of Progress County Schools but he hadn't stayed there. He'd gone back to school after he completed four years as superintendent and earned his doctorate in educational administration. He had been superintendent in four other school districts and had lived all over the country including stints in California, New York, Oregon and Alaska. When he retired he came back home, bought a house on the lake and was thoroughly enjoying kayaking and fishing and living a non-stressful life. Was that about to change?

He had an opponent in the election but Mark's name recognition and experience helped him win the election with 80% of the vote even though he spent virtually no money and little time on his campaign. The two incumbent members of the board running for reelection both lost so almost half of the school board now consisted of new members.

Mark thought that wasn't all bad even though multiple incumbents losing reelection bids is a strong signal of public dissatisfaction with the board operations. What he knew about the other two new school board members caused him to believe that the potential of the board would, at the very least, be greater than it was before. He certainly was committed to doing everything in his power to develop that potential.

At 1 p.m. today he and the other two new members were to show up at the courthouse to be sworn in as public servants. Superintendent Lindell Sharp had organized a reception after the swearing-in ceremony and had managed to get about 100 people, including most of the county's elected officials, to promise to show up for the occasion.

Mark was a bit surprised that most of the people he talked with at the reception already had some special request to make of him. Sue Melton wanted him to look into the services for special education students. She warned him that the board could be sued because the county's special education program did not measure up to federal guidelines.

Boyd Wheeler urged him to put a high priority on the quality of coaches hired at Progress County High School-especially the football coaches. He said that he'd been studying the talent at the school and concluded that the football talent at the school was superior to that of any of the opponents on the schedule last year. He said that many people in the community judged the quality of the school by its sports program. He pointed out that sports got more media coverage than all the rest of the activities at the school put together. He concluded his remarks by reminding Mark that there really is no excuse for not having winning teams boasting that his motto is anything worth doing is worth doing right.

John Wisdom, long-time County Commissioner, told Mark how happy he was to have him on the board because he knew that he would bring fiscal responsibility to the board. He expressed concern about the haphazard way that school building projects were handled and he had no doubt that significant sums of money were not being spent wisely. He cited examples that, if true, seemed to illustrate his point of view.

Margie McBee, the education reporter on the Daily News Journal, shared her concern that school board decisions far too often seemed to have been made in private discussions and not in school board meetings. She said that she had no evidence of when or how a majority of the board deliberated in private but, it was obvious to her that a majority of the board had worked things out before the meeting. She said that she did not believe that Superintendent Sharp was a party to such shenanigans. She stressed that she was very hopeful that Mark would help to change that.

Even to a seasoned educator such as Mark, it was a bit surprising that one after another, most of his well-wishers couldn't wait to share their expectations for change on the local school board.

Jerry Stubbs, another newly elected board member, told Mark that he was convinced that the board needed a new leader. He said he'd been watching Don Cameron, president of the board for the past two years, and he was committed to finding better leadership for the board. He said that the board was fortunate to have a person with Mark's experience on the board and he hoped Mark would be willing to accept the presidency.

Jerry was the owner of Stubbs Hardware Store. He'd inherited it from his uncle. He was both well-known in the community and well liked. He was the father of four children, three of whom were students in Progress County Schools. All three were gifted athletes, as was his daughter who had graduated two years earlier after setting the school scoring record in basketball. Mark thought that Jerry was intelligent, well-intentioned and committed to doing what he thought was best for children. He was known for in-depth discussions on the hardware business, the weather, and high school sports. Mark speculated that Jerry had only limited knowledge of educational issues but the community gave him high marks for character.

The third new member of the school board, Susan Goss had told Mark that she was excited to be on the school board. She said that she hoped to see significant changes on the board. She said that she had a vested interest in working for improvements in the schools because she had three children in elementary school.

Mark did not know Susan well. He knew that she was well educated and that she had been President of Ellis Elementary School PTA. He was a bit surprised when she casually mentioned to him that she thought that if the board was to make the progress she hoped for, it needed to select a good president and that he would be her choice.

Later that evening, Mark asked Maggie, his wife of forty-three years. "Do I want to be president of the school board?"

"I'm not sure that you really wanted to be on the school board and I seriously doubt that you want to be board president, especially in your first year," Maggie replied.

She had questioned why Mark wanted to be on the school board several weeks earlier before he had decided to throw his hat in the ring. She had asked, "Don't you think it will completely change our lifestyle if you are elected to the school board?" When Mark agreed that it might, she asked, "Why would you want to serve on the school board anyway?" Now, she was asking why he would consider being Board President?

"If I'm going to be on the school board," Mark responded. "I might as well be the president. It would take very little more time to be president of the board than to be just a member. I could at least move the meetings along, keep the board focused and have considerable influence on the board's agenda."

"When you were a superintendent have I heard you say many times that the work of the school board is for lay people and that if a task requires educational expertise it isn't a responsibility of the school board," Maggie reminded him. "Now, why don't you let one of the lay people be president of the board? Why don't you at least discuss it with Larry? He'll have some good advice." He responded, "At this point, I'm not planning to either seek nor accept the board presidency but I will follow your suggestion and discuss it with Larry. It wouldn't hurt anything to hear his thinking on the issue. He promised me that if I got elected to the board he'd be there for me anytime I wanted to talk about any issue."

Larry Houston was a former teacher, principal, supervisor and superintendent who had served 14 years as Executive Director of the State School Boards Association. He'd retired three years ago and had come back to his hometown to live. He'd worked with some great school boards as a superintendent and at least one that definitely could not be classified as such. He'd been to hundreds of school board meetings and conducted all kinds of seminars and workshops for school board members. He was still a popular speaker at educational meetings and he led occasional workshops and retreats for school boards. He and Mark had been friends for more than twenty years. They had worked together and Mark valued his opinions and fully expected to benefit from and draw heavily upon his judgment.

Mark wasn't surprised that Larry made an argument for both sides of this issue. He began by making the same point that Maggie had made that the work of the school board was work for lay people. He even warned that sometimes former educators didn't make good school board members because they wanted to use their professional expertise and tended to be unduly influenced by professional relationships rather than viewing issues from the position of a lay citizen. Then, he surprised Mark by informing him that he was now officially a layperson.

He reminded Mark that sometimes it's easier for a member of the board to raise issues and make points than it is for the president of the board to do so. He suggested that in this case where three school board members were former educators, public perception issues might make it more important to elect a lay person without a background in education to preside over the board meetings. On the other hand, Larry was quick to point out that the school board president has an enormous influence on how effective the board will be. He said that he had, more than once, witnessed an effective board president lead a previously dysfunctional board to become an excellent board. "Don't elect someone who can't do the job," Larry said. "An incompetent or an inefficient president pretty well destines the board to be ineffective." He suggested that Mark support another member for president, if and only if, he could find one capable of doing the job well. If not, he advised that it would be better for Mark to serve.

Mark spent some time considering the qualities and capabilities of the other school board members. He judged Michael Garcia to be a person capable of leading the board and determined that he would like to nominate him. Michael was an articulate and intelligent young man who had already earned the respect of those who knew him best. He was an immigrant whose family had moved to the United States from Honduras the year before Michael was born. His parents had later become citizens, very good citizens. Mark wanted to talk to Michael about becoming board chairman but the state's sunshine law required that board members not deliberate toward a decision outside a school board meeting and he feared that technically such a discussion might be deliberating toward a decision. He didn't want to take the risk so he would just surprise everyone at the board meeting--including Michael--with his nomination.

Mark's Reflection

Mark set aside some time that evening to reflect on a very busy day. As he considered the comments he had received from both community members and school board members, he realized that they had high expectations for him. He had sought the position and now he was going to have to do whatever it takes to help to build board effectiveness. He was confident that his decision to nominate Michael to officially lead the board was the correct one. He thought that the confidence in him expressed by some of the other board members meant that he would have an unofficial leadership role. This might be more of a challenge than he expected but he was excited by the challenge. He decided that he must be careful to avoid proclaiming educational expertise because of degrees earned or his accomplishments as an educational administrator. He must remember that being a school board member was a job for a lay person and as Larry had reminded him, that is what he now is. He should never assume that he is better qualified for the job than other board members.

Questions for Discussion

1. Why would a busy citizen even consider serving as a board member?
2. What's a good balance between trying to persuade others and listening to other views?
3. Larry said. "An incompetent or an inefficient president pretty well destines the board to be ineffective." Why do you agree or disagree with the statement?
4. Why is the job of a school board member designed for lay citizens?
5. What can Mark do to be a leader on the board without being president?

CHAPTER 2

Selecting the Board President

DON CAMERON CALLED the school board meeting to order and welcomed the members – especially the new ones. Don was into pomp and circumstance and he certainly was going to use this occasion to do what he liked best: make flowery speeches about people who may or may not be worthy of his comments.

He wanted to be re-elected as president of the board and a few well-chosen words and exaggerated compliments might influence one of the new school board members to vote for him. Although, according to his calculations, he already had the necessary votes from the returning members.

Mark had determined he wasn't going to vote for Don largely because he thought that he had used the board meetings to bring attention to himself rather than keeping the focus on the work of the school board.

"The first item of business on our agenda tonight is the election of a Board President," Don declared.

"I nominate Michael Garcia," Mark quickly announced.

"I was going to nominate you, Mark," Michael responded. "You have the experience and the expertise to be an outstanding leader for the board."

"Thanks, but I respectfully decline. I don't think we should have an educator presiding over the board this year, maybe never," Mark said. He glanced around the board table and continued, "I think that Michael can work well with each member of the board and he can lead us to become an even better board."

Ron York nominated Don for re-election but the three new members and Sylvia voted for Michael. Michael abstained and Don voted for himself. Don was visibly shaken by the outcome of the election.

"I appreciate your confidence in me," Michael informed the board. "I don't think I'm necessarily the member who is most qualified to be president of the board. However, I pledge to do my very best to make our board meetings efficient and our board as effective as possible. I welcome your suggestions as to how I might be an effective board president and I urge you to let me know when you are concerned about my leadership or lack thereof. In order for us to get to know one another better and become a more cohesive unit, I feel that it's very important for our board to spend some time discussing how we need to operate and how we can be most effective. I'm confident that every member of the board wants our board to be effective. I think a step in that direction is to hold a retreat in the very future to give us a chance to explore how we can best work together.. I will discuss this with our superintendent as soon as possible and begin exploring some possibilities. We'll bring a proposal to the board for your con-sideration and possible action."

After the meeting, Don pulled Mark aside and asked why he did not support him as president of the board. "Was it because you think the job of president should be rotated among the members?"

"No! I think it's a major mistake to select the president by rotation. The board should choose the person most capable of serving the board as president. The effectiveness of a board is tremendously affected by the leadership skills of the board president. Most good school board members just do not have the skills needed to be president of the board. I think Michael will do an excellent job," Mark said with confidence.

"Better than me?" asked Don.

"Better in the sense that he won't use the board meetings to bring attention to himself. Two incumbent members of the board were not reelected. That's a strong sign that the public wants major change on this board. You have a great deal to offer as a member of this board and I hope that you will take that as a challenge. Let's all commit to becoming a better board and get a fresh start with Michael as president. He'll do everything in his power to make the board the best it can be," Mark replied without hesitation." I believe that he is in a better position to bring the board together and help us develop into an effective, cohesive unit."

Don didn't like what he heard but he recognized that Mark didn't mind being upfront and brutally honest with him. "I hope he does well," Don said almost as if obliged to say so. "Our board will be facing a number of important issues in the next few months and we can't afford to mess them up. It could be overwhelming for an inexperienced president."

"I'm sure we'll be fine," Mark responded, "if we all work together to support and encourage Michael. Your knowledge and experience can be a big help if you'll use it to make the board better."

Shortly after Mark arrived home, the telephone rang. It was Michael Garcia, the new school board president calling. He thanked Mark for nominating him but asked why he did so. "I thought you were the best qualified to serve in that role," Mark said.

Michael responded, "I'm not even completely sure that I understand the role of the board president. Don is the only board president that I have actually observed and honestly, I don't want to follow his example. He seemed to push the board into being a divided board by pitting one member against another." Then after a brief pause, he continued, "May I ask, what are your expectations of me?"

"I expect you to preside at our meetings, keep us on target, be certain that members understand the issues we're voting on, provide ample opportunity for each board member to speak on issues but limit extraneous comments and discussion and allow for staff and community participation in meetings limited, of course, to what is relevant and helpful to the board discussion," Mark responded. "And on top of that, I expect you to do whatever else you can do to help our board be efficient and effective."

"Oh, is that all?" Michael asked jokingly.

"No," Mark responded, "that's not all, but it's a good start. I was pleased to hear you suggest a school board retreat. I was also pleased that you promised to come to the board with a proposal that you and Lindell have developed. I think that indicates clearly that you are committed to help us to become a better board and that you intend to start immediately. That's why I nominated you."

Mark smiled as he hung up the phone. He felt certain that he'd made the right decision in nominating Michael and he believed that Michael would grow in the job. He was encouraged to see evidence that Michael was open to suggestions - a quality that Mark believed to be essential for a good school board president.

Mark's Reflection

In reflecting on the board meeting, Mark was both pleased and encouraged. As one who believes in and practices reflection, he realized that one can reflect on what has happened (Past) ; what is happening (Present); and what will happen (Future). His interaction within the community and election results made it clear that the public expected more from the Board. The voters elected 3 new members and the Board elected a new President. That was a helpful, though not sufficient, beginning. The meeting was not pleasant for Don and indicated that he was not viewing his leadership from the same perspective as the others. The nominations and vote were handled in an efficient and respectful way. Mark thought that his honest and forthright conversations with Don and with Michael were consistent with the style of operation that he sought for the Board. Michael's suggestion of a retreat and his asking for suggestions from fellow members for ways to improve efficiency bode well for progress ahead. It was a good day!

Questions for discussion.

1. Why is the selection of president of the board such a critical decision?
2. Why should the board presidency not be used to honor long service?
3. Why might some very good board members not do well as President?
4. What five qualities are most important in a board president?
5. Why do you agree or disagree with Mark's decision not to be president?

CHAPTER **3**

The School Board Retreat

MICHAEL ACTED PROMPTLY. With the assistance of Superintendent Sharp, he had developed a detailed proposal and presented it at the next board meeting. After Michael responded to several questions, including Don's questions which seemed to Mark to be posturing and mumbling about why he had not scheduled a retreat when he was chairman, the board voted unanimously to participate in the retreat.

All seven members showed up on time for the retreat at Lazy River Falls State Park. The park was less than an hour away but it was a perfect place for a retreat. It had adequate meeting facilities, a very good restaurant with a beautiful view of the lake, comfortable rooms where board members could spend the night and since it was a state park, there was little chance that the board would be accused of extravagance.

Education reporter, Margie McBee was there with her iPad much to the disappointment of some of the members of the board. Margie was not unpopular with board members. She was consistently fair in her reporting. They had just hoped that they could talk without fear of being quoted. When Margie was around, most board members felt that it was necessary to be much more guarded in what they said and how they said it. They had hoped to be able to speak much more freely at this retreat.

Michael sincerely expressed his appreciation to the members of board for unanimously voting to have the retreat and for showing up on time ready to get to work. He gave a brief overview of the agenda and promptly got down to business. "We have a full and challenging agenda and I'm asking each board member to stay fully engaged for the entire board retreat." Michael began."Please turn off your cell phones and give your undivided attention to the important issues we're going to discuss today and tomorrow. We'll have breaks so you can make and return telephone calls and text messages but please try to stay focused every minute of the retreat. I believe that each item on our agenda is critical to the success of this board and anything less than total involvement by every board member will not produce the results we need. If you are willing to commit to that, please raise your hand." He was a bit hesitant to push that hard but he was pleased to see every board member lift a hand and make that commitment.

Then Michael introduced Larry Houston as the facilitator for the board retreat. He suggested that he had been told by knowledgeable people that there was no better facilitator for school board retreats in the country than Larry. He said that Larry had facilitated more than 100 school board retreats, including retreats in more than 20 states. "Suffice it to say he's good and he's here and we're fortunate to have him," Michael concluded, "So, let's get down to work."

"Wow!" Mark thought. He liked the way Michael had begun the retreat. His expectations immediately increased. He was even more encouraged as Larry began the first topic on the agenda by asking each board member to tell why he or she ran for the school board and what he or she hoped to accomplish on the board. "Now, this is going to be fun," he thought, "but it's also going to provide some useful information about where each of us is coming from."

Don volunteered to start. "I ran for the school board because many of my friends and neighbors insisted that I do so," he said. "I suppose they thought as an educator I could bring some professional expertise to the board and perhaps I would be better equipped to influence other members of the board to do things that would be best for our schools."

Mark just could not let that pass. "Don, you know that I'm a retired educator also. That's why I think I can say what I'm about to say. With all due respect, I want to point out that our entire certificated staff was chosen for their professional expertise. That's not a commodity that our school system lacks. Like you, I believe that I have some educational expertise. However, I plan to be certain that it is not a handicap for my service on the school board," he said calmly, although he was inwardly trying to control his irritation with Don's comment.

Don bristled and started to speak but before he could do so, Sylvia Taylor added, "For those of you who don't know, I've been on the board for six years now and I'm also a retired teacher." Then, she looked squarely at Mark and said, "Mark, I'm shocked by your suggestion that educational expertise might be a handicap to board service. I know that you would not make that statement without some strong basis for doing so. I'm eager to hear you elaborate on your statement. I want to think about it more deeply, but I'll have to admit, there have been issues before the board when I voted from a teacher's perspective rather than from a lay citizen's perspective. Is that the kind of thing you meant?"

"This is a fascinating discussion and I'd really like to let it continue but we need to hear from the other members as to why they ran for the board," Larry interjected. "I'm going to ask that we allow each member to respond to the question without interruption. I'll give you a chance to comment when everyone has had the opportunity to say why he or she ran, and don't forget to also share with us what you hope to accomplish as a member of the board."

"Speaking of not having much luck," Sylvia Taylor volunteered. "I ran for the board because I wanted to make our schools better places for children to learn. I also felt that this board needed an African American so that segment of our population would not feel disenfranchised. I didn't run just because I wanted just the schools in my district to be better, I wanted all of our schools to be better. I still want us to have a stronger curriculum and I want our schools to have the best teachers in the state. This is my sixth year on the board and although I have asked repeatedly, I haven't yet been able to get the board involved in any serious discussion about goals for improving our teaching staff or the curriculum in our schools. I've never been able to get either topic on the board agenda. I'm very frustrated. I think this board can and should make a difference but I don't think we have done it so far."

Totally ignoring Larry's request not to interrupt, Don said defensively, "Everything we've discussed in the six years you've been on the board has been about making our schools better places for children." He continued, " We don't hire teachers and we don't establish the curriculum. Sounds like you might want to be the superintendent rather than a school board member," he snapped sarcastically.

"I don't want to be the superintendent," Sylvia calmly objected. "I just want our board to talk about important things that we should focus on to make our schools better. Most of the things we've discussed since I've been on the board have not been sufficiently important to deserve the time of seven citizens elected to be the school board for our community. When we talk and talk but do very little, we're failing our children and the citizens who voted for us."

"So you are not pleased with what you've accomplished in the six years you've been on the school board?" Larry inquired.

"For certain, I am not!" said Sylvia. "A school board member should at least be able to get the board to consider important issues. I hope that sometime during this retreat you will tell me how I can accomplish this."

"I'd like for us to explore some possibilities including an annual agenda that might help with that," Larry replied. "But I hope you'll allow us to wait until tomorrow to explore that topic."

Sylvia nodded. "That's fine with me. If I learn nothing but how to do that, this retreat will be worthwhile for me."

"And you, Mark," Larry inquired. "Why did you run and what do you hope to accomplish?"

"I ran because I wanted to help the school board paint a picture of what our school district would be like if it were exactly what we wanted it to be," Mark said. "And, I hope to be able to participate with the board in developing a system to guide behavior of the board, staff and community as we become what we want to become. It excites me to think about the possibilities and I can hardly wait to explore them."

"You're going to have to break that down into simpler terms, Mark," Ron York said. " You're a little over my head-and besides, I'm not much of a painter."

"I think you'd look good in a painter's outfit, Ron, "Larry joked. "I think we can find a paintbrush that'll fit your hand. Mark, do you want to respond to Ron's request?"

"Sure, I'm hoping that the board will spend considerable time discussing exactly what we want our schools and school district to become," Mark replied. "Some people call it vision but I chose to describe it as painting a picture of what we want our schools to become because I think what we can see clearly in our minds, we can achieve. I'm pretty much asking for the same things Sylvia described. I want us to think about and talk a lot about what we want our schools to become." Mark continued, "I also think that it's important that we define through policy, how our school board, as well as our students, staff and community will need to behave if we are to become what we want to become." Then, he added, "I believe this board can agree on many things we want for our schools. If we can do that, we can work together to achieve those things. I want the board to focus on what we agree on instead of spending our time disagreeing."

"This is a rich discussion and we'll resume it a little later," Larry said. "Much of this retreat is going to focus on exactly what Mark mentioned. This topic is scheduled on our agenda. We can look forward to that discussion later. Let's finish our discussion on why you ran for the board. Who'll volunteer to be next?"

Jerry Stubbs raised his hand slightly as if he were still in school. He waited until Larry recognized him and then began to speak. "A primary reason that I ran for the school board was to be certain that we spend money wisely. I'm pleased to join Sylvia and Michael in making our board more colorful and more representative of our community but that was not my primary reason for running. As most of you know, I have a little business of my own. I know in order for me to survive I have to get a dollar's worth of goods for every dollar I spend. I think every governmental agency should do exactly the same. We all know that schools are not adequately funded so we have to make every penny count. I see myself as sort of a watchdog for frugality. I bark loudly when I think money is not being spent wisely."

"I think that you will find that this board has a high level of awareness of our financial accountability," Don said. "It was a high priority for me during the two years that I served as president of the board, although I suspect that some members of the board won't appreciate your barking, we'll know why you're doing it and I promise you that I will appreciate it."

Mark suspected that Jerry planned to make a greater contribution to the board than barking. He was enjoying considering whether there was anything positive about a barking school board member when Larry broke his train of thought by asking Jerry, "Do you plan to do your barking in a school board meeting or to the media?"

"Both," Jerry responded without hesitation.

"I think this issue requires further discussion and I promise we won't get away without revisiting it," Larry said as he made a note on his ipad.

"Do you consider barking to be your primary contribution to the board?" Larry asked, drawing a chuckle from the other members of the board.

"I suppose so," Jerry laughed. "But I'll do my best to contribute in other ways. I especially want our system to have good school buildings and to take good care of them and I want us to have strong sports programs for the kids."

Larry asked Susan Goss if she was ready to share.

"I have two children in the school system," Susan said. "I want to make sure that every decision made by this board is made for the benefit of children. Schools exist for children and I see myself as a champion for them. My goal is to make every decision for the benefit of our students and to challenge other board members to do the same."

Don, slightly annoyed by her remarks, challenged, "Susan, we're all champions for children! You've been to several school board meetings in the last few months, have you seen the school board make any decision that you thought was not in the best interest of children?"

"I regret to say that I have, Mr. Cameron," Susan replied. "I could cite several examples but I don't think it would serve any useful purpose. I believe that our board needs to look to the future and not to the past if we are to become, to use Mark's words, 'what we want to become.' "

That explanation did not satisfy Don, but Larry cut off discussion before he could defend the actions of the board under his leadership. "Let's hear from Ron," he said.

Ron York was the longest-serving school board member. He was beginning his fifteenth year of service on the board. He had a son who had graduated from the local high school and three children still in the school system. His wife, an elementary school secretary, had worked in the system for 22 years.

"I first ran fourteen years ago because I wanted to do what I could to put discipline back in our schools. I also wanted to put prayer back in the schools with it. I thought the two should go together so kids could pray that they didn't get a whipping," Ron joked. "Seriously, I think that we're too easy on our kids today. I hoped to help this board take the lead in challenging our schools to step up and provide the discipline that parents seem to ignore."

"Do you consider yourself to be a two-issue school board member?" Larry asked.

"Not at all," Ron replied. "I'm interested in everything that comes before the board. You asked me why I ran. That's why I ran, but I'll have to admit, I haven't had much luck in doing anything about it."

"I ran for re-election to the board at my wife's urging," Ron continued. "I wanted our system to have the best school buildings, the best teachers and the best opportunities for our students, including the best sports programs. That's why I ran for re-election to the school board and why I continue to serve."

"How do you feel about your service on the board?" Larry asked. " Do you think that you've helped this system to have the best of all those things?"

"I'm not satisfied with where we are, but we're getting there." Ron said. "I think we've made progress every year since I've been on the board."

"I don't mean to disrespect the previous board," Susan said. "But, if the system's been getting steadily better for 14 years," she inquired in earnest, "shouldn't we be the best, at least in some of those things? I think we're a long, long way from where we need to be."

"I agree with Susan," Michael chimed in. "I ran for the board because I want this system to be a great place for students to learn and grow. I don't believe our board has done bad things in the two years that I've served on it, but honestly, I don't think we've had much of an impact one way or the other. Unfortunately, our schools are not noticeably better because of the board. I can't think of anything that we've initiated. I strongly believe that our board can and must have a positive impact on our school system in a major way. We just have to figure out how to do it. I believe that it is imperative that we become a cohesive board where we listen to each other and respect each other. That's why I'm excited about this retreat. I hope we'll commit ourselves - individually and collectively- to making our schools great places to learn and great places to work."

"I can't help but believe that all of us want our schools to be great places for students to learn and we want them to continuously improve, Mark said. "As Michael said, we have to figure out how to accomplish that. Perhaps we should narrow our focus to one or two big things—things that if we corrected or did well would have a huge impact on the effectiveness of our school district."

Sylvia agreed, "I fear that our board has not had a clear and compelling vision of what we needed to do. I'd like to see our board spend more time on such an effort. What do you think, Lindell?"

Lindell responded, "I would welcome that. I have suggested such an effort in the past but there has been little enthusiasm for such an effort."

"I regret to tell you that our time has expired for this session," Larry said. "This is an important discussion that we'll continue in a later session. I can't let Susan's comment about the previous board pass without pointing out that this board is the same board as last year or even ten years ago," Larry said emphatically. "The membership is different but it's the same board. The current members have to recognize that past actions of the board--whether good or bad--were actions of this board. You own the past actions of the school board and you must live with the decisions and the policies that have been made until the board acts to change them."

Mark's Reflection

As Mark reflected on the discussions of the board at the retreat, he concluded that the board members had begun to realize that, for the most part, they all wanted the same things for the students in their district. He was pleased to conclude that members of the board, although extremely different in personality and capability, had more in common than in their differences. He would accept the challenge to do what he could to help the board lead in a single direction even when the members disagree strongly on how to get where they want to go.

He thought that his terminology of the board painting a picture of what it wanted to become was generally well received. But when he thought of Ron's comments, he recognized that it will require a major effort to get the board to agree to spend the time needed and to muster the enthusiasm for painting a picture of how the board wants its schools and school district to look. He was not completely sure that "painting a picture" was better than "setting a vision," but thought it was acceptable.

It was becoming more clear to him that members differ greatly on whether the better way for the board to do its work is to focus on becoming the system we want to be or eliminating the things we do not want in our system. It could be a useful tool for clarification:1) creating more of what we want or 2) getting rid of what we don't want. Perhaps it would be useful to discuss the two approaches when there is no issue in the pipeline. Are the two approaches mutually exclusive or could they be complimentary? Another thought entered his mind about a board being judged in part for the unwanted things that have been allowed to continue.

He smiled as he reflected on Sylvia's strong explanation of the board as a corporate body. He decided that somehow, every member needed to buy into that notion if the board were to have significant achievements. His experience led him to believe that the words we use to think and talk about the board are very important and give us our first clue about how we see the board. Sylvia used "corporate body." He liked what that said about how she thought the board should function.

He decided that he should complement Sylvia for articulating her position so well and so persuasively. In fact, he thought that after each meeting, he would make it a practice to compliment people who contributed to the success of the meeting. He would demonstrate an attitude of gratitude.

He determined that he would be positive, supportive and upbeat about the work of the board. He believed this board had a shot at greatness.

As he thought of things members could do to promote unity, it occurred to him that he should deal with the irritation he felt for Don and some of his comments. He would be more considerate of him. The remark by Don about influencing other board members reminded him of a conversation and a quote from Catherine Epstein. He looked it up to refresh his memory: "Hearing and understanding means resisting the urge to persuade, which seems both radical and uncomfortable." Tough challenge, he thought. There were more things on which to reflect...on another day.

Questions for discussion

1. Why would you want to know reasons other members chose to serve?
2. What metaphors or models for the board effectively speak to you?
3. Why is it beneficial for a board to develop a trust relationship with media representatives who cover the board? Are all discussions and reports "on the record?"
4. Explain the significance of the board being a corporate body?
5. How could educational expertise be a handicap to board service?

CHAPTER 4

Being An Effective Member Of The School Board

"WHAT IS AN effective school board member?" Larry asked to begin the next session of the retreat.

"It is a person who knows what the people in his district want to be done in their schools and he gets it done," Ron said.

"That is exactly what I was thinking," Jerry said, but Ron said it better than I would have said it. And to be perfectly honest," he continued, "I almost didn't run for a seat on the school board because I'm not sure that I know enough about education and schools to be a good school board member. I want to contribute to the board but I don't have the educational background and experience that some of you have."

"Thanks for sharing those comments, Jerry," Larry responded. Then, he asked the group, "Would you rather vote for a school board candidate who claims to have all the answers or one who has questions and issues that he or she is committed to solving by working with other board members, school administrators and the community?"

Michael responded, "I believe that you have raised a critically important question. I have never thought a candidate for any office, including the school board, should be expected to have all the answers. I suspect that a candidate who thinks that he or she has all the answers would be less likely to solicit, or even listen to, the ideas of others who may very well have better ideas. It seems logical that the collective thinking of all of us together is likely to be superior to the ideas of any one of us."

"I agree," Mark added. "I appreciate Jerry's honesty and openness about his concerns. I think that it's important that we all acknowledge that educational expertise is not a requirement for school board members. I remind you that being a school board member is the job of a lay person. Much more important is willingness to listen and learn, to work cooperatively to create a plan to make our schools and school system great places to work and learn." Then, he looked straight at Jerry and said, "Jerry, I have no doubt that you're going to be a board member who will make our community proud."

"I couldn't agree more." Susan observed. "I think we all have high expectations for Jerry."

After a brief pause, Susan said, "I'd like to go back to Ron's definition of a good school board member. I have a problem with his definition that a good school board member knows what the people in his district want and knows how to get it done. I believe that an effective school board member is equally concerned with issues in all districts in the school system, not just the district from which he or she was elected."

"People in all districts don't elect you. People in your district do. If you don't do what they want, you'll never serve on the school board for fourteen years as I have done." Ron retorted.

"I agree with Susan. We're elected by voters in our district but we represent all of the students in our school system. However, I don't believe that an effective school board member is consistently guided by what the public wants," Sylvia said. "Too often, I've seen the majority want something that was not necessarily good for the school district."

"So have I," Susan added. "The public does not have as much information as we have. We go to workshops and other meetings. We receive briefings from the superintendent and staff. We have an opportunity to interact with each other and with people directly involved in the issues. Certainly, we aren't supposed to forget all that we know and vote for whatever citizens favor. I certainly think that knowing in advance "what the system or any part of it needs" is secondary to being a good listener and an effective decision-maker who can work as a team with those who "see it differently than I."

Larry walked to the whiteboard and wrote,

**School board members do not react to public
opinion, they create it.**

He asked, "Who agrees with this statement?"

"I think it's right on," Mark said. "When citizens come to us to share their opinions, we should listen but we also have a responsibility to help them understand the issue from our perspective. If the board has already decided on the issue, we should help our citizens to understand the board's perspective. When we do this, we create public opinion."

"That's a totally new concept for me," Michael confessed. "I never thought of myself as having a responsibility to create public opinion, but I love the statement, 'Board members don't react to public opinion, they create it.' It makes sense and it gives us a powerful leadership responsibility. Besides, the idea of creating public opinion excites me."

"I need to think about the concept some more," Sylvia added. "At first blush, I like it and it strikes me that it could be both fun and an important leadership role."

"Write it down and think about it." Larry urged, Then, he erased it and wrote on the board:

AN EFFECTIVE SCHOOL BOARD MEMBER

Studies the issues and votes for what
he/she thinks is best for all students

"Are we all in agreement that this is one quality of an effective school board member?" Larry asked. All members either said "yes" or nodded their heads in agreement.

"I certainly agree with the statement," said Mark, "but I don't believe it's enough for a school board member to simply vote for what he or she thinks is right."

"What more should we be expected to do," asked Susan.

Mark replied, "I believe that the best school board members prepare themselves to articulate their positions in a persuasive manner. Good board members should accept responsibility when they lose a vote to acknowledge that they did not present their position in a sufficiently effective manner."

"I propose," Mark continued, "that we add the phrase, "and presents positions to the board in a thoughtful, persuasive manner. So, it would read: Studies the issues and votes for what he/she thinks is best for all students and presents positions to the board in a thoughtful, persuasive manner."

"I support that wholeheartedly," Sylvia said. "Honestly, I have sometimes placed the blame on fellow board members for being too dull to understand my position. I think it is more productive if I place blame on myself and recognize that I, not they, am the one who has not been bright enough to get the job done."

"It does my heart good to hear Sylvia admit that," Don joked. "I have often felt that she included me among the "dull" members of the board. Let's add the phrase that Mark proposed so I can from henceforth, forevermore blame Sylvia when I vote against her motions."

Sylvia laughed politely along with most of the board but she didn't reply.

Larry asked for a show of hands of those who supported the addition. It was unanimous. So, he added:

Studies the issues and votes for what he/she thinks is best for all students and presents positions to the board in a thoughtful, persuasive manner

"Before we move on Larry, why did you erase the previous statement about board members creating public opinion," Michael inquired. "I think it is an important quality of an effective school board member. I suggest that you add as number two: Creates rather than reacts to public opinion."

"I agree," Susan added. "I had never thought about it that way but I like it very much. I think it could change the way we view our interaction with the public. We need to spend time educating our community about issues the board is facing. In my opinion, that one idea makes this retreat a success."

"Are you suggesting that we're creating public opinion every time we educate the community about an issue," Don asked.

"That is precisely what I'm suggesting," Michael replied. "Think about it. Whenever we learn something new or gain information we did not previously have, it changes our understanding of the subject which amounts to changing our opinion of the issue."

"How do the rest of you feel about that?" Larry asked. Again, all members either said "yes" or nodded their heads in agreement. Sylvia added, "This is a concept that I've never heard before and one that didn't occur to me. But it will make a major difference in the way I consider public opinion." She continued, "If I didn't get anything from this retreat except this, it would be worth being here."

So, Larry wrote on the whiteboard::

Creates rather than reacts to public opinion

"I think a good school board member is respectful of the opinions of other school board members however stupid they may appear," Jerry volunteered. "I realize that I don't have the experience that some members of the board have and I don't have the knowledge about educational issues that other members of the board have. However, I was elected by the voters in my district and I hope that I can feel free to express my opinion without being either ignored or ridiculed." Then, he added, "It's fine to disagree with me, just don't ignore me or treat me like I'm stupid."

Ron added, "I have felt disrespected many times by other board members in the past. It hurt me and made me not want to share my opinions but I usually ended up saying what I wanted to say only when I was angry and just couldn't be quiet anymore."

Larry wrote on the whiteboard:

**Respects the opinions of other members of the board
and works in a collaborative manner with them.**

"Can we accept that?" he asked. All members nodded in agreement.

"I think we should add, "Respects, supports, and expresses appreciation to the superintendent and staff for their work," Sylvia suggested.

"I can't support the superintendent or the staff in everything they do," Ron objected. "We wouldn't need a school board if we're going to be a rubber stamp."

"I am not suggesting that we support the superintendent or the staff in everything they do," Sylvia replied. "What I'm suggesting is that we recognize the work of our superintendent and staff and that we tell them from time to time how much we appreciate what they do. I'm also suggesting that we support their efforts. I believe that every member of this board wants what's best for our school district and the children it serves. I believe the same is true for the superintendent and staff. We will sometimes disagree on issues but we should be supportive of each other because we share the same major goal."

"Thanks for expressing that, Sylvia," Michael said. "I couldn't agree more. I think that an attitude of mutual respect, support and appreciation will be an enormous enabler of our board moving toward effectiveness."

Larry wrote on the Smartboard:

Respects, supports and expresses appreciation to the superintendent and staff for their work

Susan raised her hand and after Larry recognized her, she asked what a school board member should do about supporting a decision of the board that the member voted against and continued to oppose. "I don't see how I can be expected to support a position that I opposed simply because the majority of the board voted for it," she continued.

"Sylvia pointed out earlier in this retreat that a majority of the public is sometimes wrong. Likewise, I think that a majority of the board could be wrong and if that happens, I don't want to feel obligated to support the decision," Susan said.

"I've never supported a decision of the board that I didn't vote for," Ron said with some element of pride. "If I'm for it, I let it be known and if I'm against it, I raise hell about it."

"Let me tell you a true story to illustrate my point," Ron continued. "Ten years ago, the board hired a hot shot professor to make a study of where an elementary school should be located. I was against hiring him in the first place and later when he made his recommendation, I told the board that he was recommending building in the wrong place. I told them where we should build the school but I was the only one who voted against his recommendation. Since the school has been built, the population growth has occurred exactly where I said we should build the school." He boasted, "I have never let the board or the community forget that I was right and the board was wrong."

"Do you feel that you made the board more effective by going about telling the community that the board made a bad decision?" Larry asked.

"No, I don't think it made the board more effective, but it sure let people know that the whole board is not a rubber stamp. It has at least one member who thinks for himself and who is not afraid to stand alone," Ron replied with a touch of arrogance in his voice.

"Do you think that reminding the community for ten years that the board that you are a part of made a bad decision enhanced public opinion of the school board?

"No, it clearly did not, Ron replied.

"Do you consider one of the responsibilities of this school board to be to provide citizen leadership for the school district," Larry asked Ron.

"Yes," Ron replied.

"Should the board's leadership result in the community getting behind the board to support the schools?" Larry asked looking directly at Ron.

"Yes," Ron replied. "The board should lead the community in supporting schools and in getting things done that should be done."

"Then, the board has to decide in what direction it will lead," Larry said. "It can't lead part of the community in the direction some members want to go and the rest of the community in the direction the majority of the board wants to go. The board leads in one direction or it doesn't lead at all. Does that make sense?"

"It makes sense," Ron admitted, "but it doesn't make sense that I should support something that I'm against. I want the board to lead but not at the expense of its members being independent individuals who speak out on issues. We were told at the last school board academy that I attended that once a decision is made, I should not tell people how I voted or what my concerns were. I disagreed then and I disagree now. How can the public have confidence in me as a board member if I refuse to discuss my own position on an issue?

"I understand what Ron is saying," Susan interrupted. "I'm not as outspoken as he is, but I don't feel comfortable having to jump aboard a train going to someplace that I don't want to go."

"No one wants to do that and I don't think the board wants you to do that," Mark reassured her. "When the board is facing an issue about which we feel strongly, we should each articulate our position in a thoughtful and persuasive manner. Then, after the vote, we must acknowledge that we were a part of the group which considered the issue and made a decision on it. Whether or not we are on the prevailing side, we should do what we can to make the decision of the board that we participated in work as best it can. If I am on the losing side, I should feel free to tell what my personal position was but I must acknowledge that I had a chance to speak out for what I believed was right. I articulated my position as persuasively as I could to my fellow board members who, like me want the best for the school district and its students. I fought a good fight but I was not able to advance an argument that was persuasive to a majority. Consequently, I will do what I can to make the board's decision work. To do otherwise would be to want the board's leadership to fail."

"I'll have to admit, that is a persuasive argument. I couldn't have said it better myself," Jerry joked. "In fact, I wouldn't have said it at all because I had never even thought about what you just said. But I'll have to say, it makes sense to me. I guess that I should, here and now commit myself to do what I can to make the decisions of this board work whether I originally supported them or not. I'm going to do my best to do that and I challenge every member of the board to do the same."

"I'll accept your challenge and join you in that commitment, Sylvia declared. Michael and Mark followed suit but Susan said she needed more time to think it through. Ron promised to think about it some more. Then, he said, "After the school was built in the wrong place, all my complaining didn't do anything to get it moved. It probably would be better if I didn't mention it anymore."

Don remained totally silent on the subject.

Larry wrote: **Accepts and supports the decisions of the board**

He suggested that he was tentatively adding the fifth quality for further thinking and consideration even though everyone had not bought into it yet. He said the list was not intended to be exhaustive. He said that given the opportunity the board could easily identify other qualities of an effective school board member. However, the time for this session was up. He challenged them to continue to think about how each of them could be effective and contribute to the success of the board. He said that the board could never achieve maximum effectiveness until each member of the board became effective.

He reminded them that the board is a corporate body and that although individual members have responsibilities to make the board effective, the board will be judged on its effectiveness as a unit. He recommended that the board participate in a session to build further on this one during which it further considers the qualities of an effective board. He adjourned the session.

During the break following the session, Mark had several discussions with individual members of the board about the session. Jerry said he had never participated in a more enlightening session. He thought that he had gained new insight into being a school board member that would serve him well in the future. Sylvia said that she was thrilled with the entire retreat. She said she had not been ready for any of the sessions to end. She was confident that the board would be a better board as a result of this retreat. Ron said he had picked up several things to think about and Don said he couldn't say that it was better than the new board member orientation that he led last year but he was not disappointed in the session. Susan said, as a new school board member, she was learning an enormous amount. She suggested that without this experience, she would have made many mistakes that she will not make now.

Mark's Reflection

Mark thought that if he had been giving the session a grade, it would have been A+. He sensed growth in the members of the board and was pleasantly surprised that board members were as receptive to new ideas as they had just demonstrated that they were. He was enthusiastic and optimistic about the future of this board. He wondered if the individual members were fully aware of the strengths that each brings to the board and how those strengths can contribute to the board.

Three members have identified their experience as educators and his remark about educational experience as plentiful in the system may have contributed to downplaying its value. Don seems proud of his experience and views it as "expertise." Sylvia referred to her experience in terms of "perspective" and cited it as a bit of a deterrent to sound decisions. We have more work to do on this one, he thought.

He recalled how Jerry's openness to his perceived weakness as a board member had produced a positive discussion that resulted in a welcome expression of confidence in him. Mark speculated that such supportive comments were building cohesiveness and acceptance within the board. He pledged to himself that he would look for opportunities to express genuine supportive or encouraging comments to other board members. His expectations for board success were growing.

Questions for discussion

1. What duty does a board member have to his/her district of representation?
2. How does that duty differ from the board member's duty to the other areas of the school district?
3. To what extent should individual qualifications of a member (e.g. a lawyer) be used in making decisions by the board?
4. Why do you agree or disagree with the statement that, "One can't be an effective member on an ineffective board?
5. Which of the qualities of an effective school board member that Larry wrote on the board do you believe is the most important? Least important? Why?

CHAPTER 5

Role Of The School Board

LARRY BEGAN THE next session of the retreat by asking participants why communities went to the trouble of electing school board members. "Or perhaps a better question is what should school boards do?" he asked.

"They run the school district," Ron said.

"I don't think so," Sylvia objected." Running the school district is a management responsibility. The board is about governance. I think it's our job not to run the schools but to see that the schools are run well."

"And how does a school board do that?" Larry asked. "On this school board, we have seven members all with varied backgrounds coming together to make up a board of education. Are you qualified to run the school system or even to see that the school system is run well?"

"Mark has been a superintendent," Ron said. 'That should count for something."

"Remember that Mark also said that he didn't want to let that be a handicap," Sylvia reminded Ron. "I'd appreciate hearing him elaborate on that a bit."

"In my opinion," Mark said," if the board is asked to do something which requires educational expertise, it's being asked to do something that is not its job. Our professional staff is filled with educators. Our board doesn't need to be filled with educators as well."

"I always considered my educational background to be an asset rather than a liability," Don said. "I don't see any way it could be a handicap to a board member."

"Don, do you agree that the job of a school board member is a job for a lay citizen?" Mark asked.

"I do agree with that, "Don replied, but that doesn't make educational expertise a handicapping condition. Does it?"

"I don't think it's a handicapping condition," Sylvia said." But it could make a board member be less open minded and consequently less effective. I appreciate Mark's warning. I've determined not to allow my educational expertise to be a handicap on this board and I invite any member to call my hand anytime you think that I'm allowing it to adversely affect my judgment. I spoke earlier about how I had allowed my perspective as a teacher to influence my vote on occasion. I need to find ways to use that perspective to improve my effectiveness; for sure, this board needs to be aware of the teacher perspective in most of its deliberations."

"I have seen a retired principal who wanted to substitute his judgment for the superintendent's judgment after he became a school board member," Don admitted, "but I'm not going to do that."

"I guess I see it a little differently," Susan said. "I hope this doesn't come out wrong but I think that the education of our young people is too important to leave to educators. I don't mean that to be a slam on educators in any way because we couldn't operate without educational expertise. I just think it's the job of the school board to provide a different perspective from the educators. We need to look at what the educators propose and see if it makes sense from the public perspective and the parental perspective. In a sense it's a system of checks and balances."

"You did not mention the student's perspective, Susan; do you think that the parent can speak for the student?" asked Jerry. "They try to, but the student perspective remains a vital one in all educational deliberations. Michael said earlier that schools should be great places to learn. I would like to see us give greater consideration to engaging students more effectively in their own learning," Susan answered.

Judging that the subject had adequately been discussed, Larry skillfully guided the attention back to what the board should be doing with its time. "Sylvia, you said you weren't happy with what the board has been spending its time on in the two years you've been on the board. What did the board do that you thought was not appropriate?"

"I think our board has largely been a rubber stamp for our superintendent," Sylvia replied." That's not intended to be a negative comment toward Lindell. I'm glad the board has confidence in him and has agreed with his suggestions but our county does not need a school board that is a rubber stamp. The board should be articulating a vision of what we want our schools to become, not just reacting to proposals from the superintendent. The superintendent deserves a board that provides a big picture of what we want our school district to become."

"You asked us to call your hand when we thought you were letting your education background interfere with your board role. I'm calling your hand. I think you are wanting to do the superintendent's job, Don objected. "This board is here to react to proposals initiated by the superintendent and staff. It's his job to propose and ours to approve or reject his proposals."

"I completely agree that we must react to proposals initiated by the superintendent and staff. I realize that it's part of our job." Sylvia responded. "I do object to the lack of initiative that I've seen on the part of our board since I've been a member. We have a responsibility to define what we want our school system to become and give our all to help it become what we've said that it should be."

Larry jumped into the conversation to say, "I had a good friend, Linton Deck, who used to say this about school boards: 'When we don't know what to do, we do what we know.' I believe that's frequently a problem with school boards. They do what they know when they don't know what to do. None of us want that to be true for this board so let's see if we can come to some agreement about what a school board should do."

"Is this why some board members want to spend a lot of time reviewing purchasing and paying bills (things that are administrative procedures) rather than considering curriculum and educational outcomes- topics with which they are less comfortable?"asked Susan of no particular person.

Ron responded immediately as if he'd been waiting for this opportunity. "I can tell you from serving 14 years on this school board that we have the hardest job of any elected public official. We have to make decisions that affect the one thing people care about most – their children-- and we have to do it right here in front of the community every day. We're not like the state legislators who go off to Nashville or the congressman who go off Washington and tell people whatever they want to hear about what great things they are doing for them. Our citizens see what we do and they don't hesitate to tell us what they think we're doing wrong."

Ignoring Ron, as she would do many more times in the future, Sylvia responded to Larry's question: "I propose that the first thing our board should do is to describe what we want our system to become. Isn't that what you were talking about, Mark when you said that we should paint a picture of what our schools and school district should look like?"

Mark nodded. "Exactly. We develop our vision by using words to paint a picture of what we want our school system to be. Some words do this much better than others."

"Can we accept that one of the jobs of the school board is to determine what it wants the system to become?" Larry asked.

Several members nodded and no one, including Don, objected. Larry wrote, "Articulate a Vision" on the smartboard. He asked if members were okay with what he had written and when everyone agreed he asked members to identify another job of the school board.

"Obviously, the board is responsible for developing policies to provide guidance for students, staff and community," Don suggested. "I don't think it's a very popular activity for our school board, but I think it's an important one."

"Why does our board need to spend a lot of time developing school board policy?" Ron asked. "Who pays any attention to school board policy anyway?"

"Maybe it's because we put things into policy that shouldn't be there," Jerry said." I was reading in our policy manual just yesterday and I was surprised at the detail included there. The board couldn't possibly enforce some of the things in our policy manual. I'd like to see us clean it up and take out everything that we can't or don't intend to enforce."

"I don't claim to be an expert in this area, Michael said, "but I think many of the policies in our manual should be identified as administrative procedures rather than policy. They are issues that administrators should decide...too detailed to be policy."

"I couldn't agree with you more," Sylvia said." It will be quite a challenge to take them out but I think we should do it. Could we ask Lindell and his staff to identify current policies that should be administrative procedures and bring them back to the board for action?"

"We'll gladly do it," Lindell said. "Just give us six weeks and we'll have a proposal ready for the board's consideration."

Larry complimented Lindell for his willingness to take on the project. He suggested that the board needed to spend a lot more time discussing its responsibility for policy development. He felt some urgency to move the discussion forward so he wrote on the smartboard: Develop policy. Then, he said: "When a board begins to understand that it's responsible to govern but not manage the school district, it is more likely to increase its focus on policy. An effective board uses the power of policy to guide the implementation of its vision describing what excellence looks like."

Larry asked members to name another responsibility of the school board.

Mark was determined not to dominate the conversation. He very much wanted to know what other board members thought and he was anxious to understand how they thought. However, he had strong feelings about the board's responsibility for community leadership. He had never seen a board understand and accept this part of its responsibility. He wanted this board to be effective more than he wanted to remain in the background so he suggested: "I think community leadership is an essential responsibility of a school board. We can't achieve an acceptable level of effectiveness unless we fulfill our responsibility for community leadership. It is one of the most enjoyable responsibilities of a school board yet, it is the most frequently neglected."

"There you go again," Ron said." I don't even know what you're talking about."

Mark was a bit disappointed that Ron seemed to be on a mission to show that he was talking over the heads of an average school board member. He felt that it was almost impossible not to talk over Ron's head when he had it buried in the sand. He wanted to tell Ron that he was intelligent enough to understand if he would listen more carefully and think before he reacted, but he didn't. He had already decided that Ron was not an average school board member and he wished that Ron could rise to that level. He wondered how Ron could've served on the school board for 14 years and know so little. "I'm not going to write him off," Mark thought, "This board cannot achieve its maximum effectiveness unless every member, including Ron, becomes effective."

He patiently responded to Ron: "I'm talking about helping our community to understand the issues that this board faces and helping them to see themselves as owners of the schools rather than customers of the schools. I'm talking about listening to our citizens and helping them to understand the thinking that goes into our decisions. I'm talking about what we discussed earlier: creating public opinion rather than reacting to it. I believe that our community will even more strongly support schools if they feel they own them and if they see that this board realizes that the schools belong to the citizens of the community. I'm talking about interacting with the county commission on a regular basis and sharing with it the issues our schools are facing. I think our board in the past has been more involved in building fences than it has been in building bridges to the county commission."

"I understand that," Ron said, "and I think that I mostly agree with you. I'll have to admit that you stepped on my toes when you were talking about our relationship with the county commission. I've said some pretty bad things about them, but I honestly think that they deserved it. I thought that I was trying to build bridges that I felt that they were burning."

Susan had been sitting quietly for a while but this discussion drew a response from her. "As I said earlier, I never thought of community leadership as a major responsibility of the school board. But, after hearing this discussion, I'm convinced that the reputation of this board would be greatly enhanced in our community if we would do what Mark described. I can see how it may well be one of the most important responsibilities of the board."

"May I add community leadership as one of the key responsibilities of the board?" Larry asked. "If you think it is, please raise your hand."

Every hand in the room went up, including the hands of Lindell Sharp and Margie McBee. Larry wrote on the smartboard: Community Leadership

Sylvia responded: "I guess that now is as good as any time to raise an issue of critical importance. It is not one around which I have expertise or knowledge of what to do, so please, do not ask me to suggest a plan. As a parent, teacher, and now board member I am increasingly aware that many of the things that our students learn are not the result of intentional learning experiences, nor even the result of social activities at our schools. Without downplaying the importance of curriculum and intentional learning opportunities, I have come to believe that much of the most powerful learning of our students is caught rather than taught. I speak of the impact of our community on what and who our young people are becoming. We can go on with our planning or we can deliberately get involved with the opportunity to provide community leadership. The community in which our schools are embedded can help or harm the growth and development of our youth. I wish that I had some profound suggestions."

Mark said, "You seem to be speaking of more than the hidden curriculum. "

"Yes," Sylvia responded. "I'm speaking of the total impact from living in our community, things this board has no control over, and little influence on unless we engage with the community in ways different from our present ones. We have churches, civic clubs, organizations, business, and some individuals who do things intended to help students. Are we looking at community leadership as influencing these folks?"

Michael wanted to be both understanding and inclusive in his response."Perhaps we should include community leadership as one of our tasks and continue to explore the profound issues raised by Sylvia."

"Where does the employment and the subsequent evaluation of a superintendent fall as a duty of the Board of Education? "Susan inquired. "That seems to me to be a management issue rather than a governance issue."

"You're exactly right," Larry responded. "You've identified an important management responsibility of the board."

"So, boards are not supposed to exist solely to govern the school district. They are involved in management also. Right?" Ron asked.

"Boards are almost exclusively about governance," Larry emphasized." But the employment and evaluation of the superintendent is an exception. It's a management responsibility because there's no one else to do it. I think that the board should look at it as an opportunity to carry out its management responsibility in such an excellent manner that it sets an example for others in the school system with management responsibilities. With your agreement, I will add Employ and Evaluate the Superintendent to the three governance functions we've listed."

Mark's Reflection

Mark was pleasantly surprised with the quality of the board's discussion on this issue. "We've talked a good game as we have been identifying board responsibilities," he thought. "Now, we've got to accept our responsibilities and carry them out in an excellent manner. That's going to be a tremendous challenge for this board. We're going to have to work hard to help each other learn that mistakes are meant for learning, not for repeating. It's definitely going to be an uphill battle but I'm anxious to get started. The issue raised by Sylvia is critically important and must be considered."

Questions for discussion

1. **How critical is the matter of casting a vision for the district? Would the vision of one district not be the same as for every other school district?**
2. **Will our vision statement focus on creating what we want but do not have yet, or what we have that we do not want? Or both? What difference will it make?**
3. **Have the decisions of state and federal governments made it more challenging for us to provide leadership? How will we respond?**
4. **Don said, "This board is here to react to proposals initiated by the superintendent and staff. It's his job to propose and ours to approve or reject his proposals." How would you respond to those statements?**

5. Sylvia said, "Running the school district is a management responsibility. The board is about governance. I think it's our job not to run the schools but to see that the schools are run well." What tools does the school board have to see that the school district is run well?

CHAPTER 6

The Retreat: Policy

LARRY REMINDED THE board of the discussion the previous day about policy. He commended the members for the quality of discussion and told them he appreciated their interest in exploring the potential benefits that policy held for the board. He said that "policy is viewed by some as the most important function of a local board of education while others describe it as the only legitimate function of a local board." He told them that he did not hold either of these views. Rather, he described policy as "a powerful tool that boards may use to guide the school community in achieving its vision."

Don observed, "Both the federal and state governments have increasingly mandated local boards to adopt specific policies on a growing number of topics. They've also taken away some of our powers through legislation. It appears that they don't have much respect for local control or for the local school board."

"There is no question that what Don has said is true but I see that as a challenge that I think our board needs to accept," Sylvia said as she walked to the smart board. She wrote in large letters on the board: WE MUST RESTORE CONFIDENCE IN OUR SCHOOL BOARD! "This is our challenge," she said emphatically. "We can use policy to help enhance the reputation and effectiveness of this board. We must stop flying by the seat of our pants. I sincerely believe that we could use policy to help bring about the changes we want in our school district."

Sylvia continued, "The state and federal governments have taken to mandating that we adopt certain policies. They've been taking away powers of local boards through legislation. It is obvious to me that neither they nor our citizens hold school boards in high esteem. If we revise our policies to include only things that will help us achieve our vision, we'll be taking a step in the direction of getting our community to have a higher regard for both policy and our board. We will use our policy to give voice to our vision."

Michael began to applaud and everyone else in the room joined in." If we all can share that kind of passion for our work," Michael said, "we'll become a great board and I don't doubt that our community will recognize it."

"I liked the speech," Ron said,"but I don't see how we can make a policy that the community has to respect us. I think that we could spend our time better by solving problems as they come up. It's a total waste of time to develop a bunch of policies about situations that may never happen."

"That's not the only thing that you don't see," Mark thought. But he resisted the urge to say it. He was still committed to doing everything he could to help Ron be a more effective school board member. Instead, he said, "Our board doesn't meet often enough to deal with situations as they arise. That's what administrators do. Policy is the board speaking when it's not convened. Board policy institutionalizes wisdom that has been developed over time. The wisdom reflected in our policy provides guidance to our administrators and helps them make better decisions as they deal with issues on a daily basis. The administration is empowered to act with confidence that it has board support because the board has provided guidance through policy. And, when the community sees evidence of the administration and the board acting as a team, its confidence in both the board and administration grows."

"How else could a lay board efficiently govern the school district?" Michael asked." It makes sense but, I'll have to admit that I had never considered policy to be quite that important. I am now persuaded that policy is a source of board power and we definitely need to take our policy responsibilities more seriously."

"I love where this discussion is going," Mark said. "I consider policy to be one of the most valuable governance tools available for boards and I find it strange that our board in the past seemed to have such a distaste for policy making."

"I'll put our policies up against any school board in the state," Don snapped." This board did not ignore policy. We stayed on top of it."

"I don't mind telling you that I don't enjoy making policy one bit," Ron admitted. "In fact, I have hated every minute that we spent on it. It seems like such a nitpicky activity. I don't like arguing over whether we use this word or that word or how we punctuate a sentence. I'm not an English teacher."

"I'm reluctant to admit it, but I agree with part of Ron's comment," Susan added. "I wish we could discuss the concepts and come to some agreement about what we want, then leave the grammar and wordsmithing to Lindell and his staff. Would that work, Lindell?"

"That's exactly how we'd like to do it," Lindell replied. "I've never suggested that the school board spend time in trying to actually write policy. It works better if the school board will tell us what you want a policy to accomplish and let us draft it for the board's consideration at the next meeting. It's much easier for the board to do minor editing to what we've worked on than to compose policy at a board meeting."

Michael reminded the board that it is in a retreat and shouldn't be voting on issues but he suggested that the board begin this process by asking Michael to draft a policy on policy making for the board's consideration at its next meeting. Lindell said the board already had such a policy but he and the staff would review it and draft changes in the policy to make it consistent with the board's discussion today.

"Let me throw out a couple of ideas for the board's consideration," Larry proposed. "I'd like to know the extent of your agreement with the following statements about policy:

> **The aim of policy is to advance the school system on a steady course toward the attainment of the board's vision. It emerges as the school board envisions the ideal operation of the school system moving toward its vision and provides guidance for those joining the effort. If a policy doesn't relate to the board's vision it shouldn't be a policy.**

"I totally agree with everything you said," Sylvia responded. Policy should help us move toward a vision and if it doesn't, it might be an administrative procedure but it is not a policy. As I've said before, our policy manual is filled with things we can't enforce and statements that are far too detailed for school board policy."

"It seems to me that most of our policies are designed to avoid or eliminate what we don't want," said Michael. "We'd be making quite a change if we decided to create policies that say what we want rather than what we forbid. The task will be more difficult and also more beneficial."

Larry reminded the board, "When the board accepts the notion that it is responsible to govern but not to manage the school district, it's more likely to increase its focus on policy and much more likely to use policy to create rather than using it to forbid." He continued, "An effective board uses the power of policy to guide the implementation of its vision. Of course, that won't work unless the board actually has a vision."

Board members seemed to be taken back by Larry's last statement. They began to consider whether their board actually had a vision. Susan raised the issue publicly. "Does our board have a vision?" she asked. "If it does, I'd like to know what it is and I'd very much like to have a chance to weigh in on it."

Don assured her that the board did, in fact, have a vision. He suggested that she read the vision statement in the policy manual. Susan seemed less than impressed. "It seems to me that there is a considerable difference between a vision statement and an actual vision," she said. "Am I wrong?"

"You are exactly right," Larry said." I can't tell you how many boards have a vision statement but no vision. Unless the board has described in compelling language what it wants the system to become, it has no vision. The most useful vision statement is one which paints a compelling word picture of what the system will look like when it is achieving its vision."

"Shouldn't we get right on that task?" Susan asked. "The Bible says that where there is no vision the people perish. I assume that is the same for school districts."

"Fortunately, we have scheduled a session on that later in the retreat," Larry said. "We can't develop the vision during that session, but we can explore and lay the foundation for the process."

As soon as Larry stopped talking, Susan said, "I have an observation and a question. I attended the last three meetings of the school board before I became a member. I was surprised at how much the board talked about things and ended up taking no action whatsoever. I never heard school board policy mentioned one time. Now I'm thinking that some of the discussions should have ended up with the board providing LIndell and the staff with ideas that led to a policy draft." She continued, "In case you didn't recognize it, that was my observation. Now my question. Shouldn't discussions of the board nearly always lead to action by the board?

Neither Susan's observation nor her question sat well with Don. He was more than a bit sarcastic in his response: "Sometimes the board just needs to talk and share individual reactions to things that have happened or may happen. As you will learn when you get more experience, policymaking is not the only responsibility of this board."

Susan resisted the urge to say, "You arrogant ass. It's no wonder you weren't re-elected as Board President." Instead, she politely said, "I didn't intend to be judging the board. It's my sincere desire that this board become the best board we can be. Our community wants to see our board governing our schools in an efficient and effective manner and our children deserve a board that does everything in its power for their benefit. I pledge to you that my questions and comments will consistently be designed toward that end. I'd like to see this board adopt a policy holding ourselves to high standards of speech and conduct as school board members. That's one way our board can achieve Sylvia's challenge to enhance the board's credibility."

Sylvia started clapping and everyone else except Don joined in. Larry looked straight at Susan and said, "Thank you, Susan. I love your passion and I love your suggestion that the board hold itself to a high standard of conduct and speech. I remind you again that an effective board uses the power of policy to guide the implementation of its vision. The word intention is consistent with vision and carries a bit less baggage. I will use it here to make the point made by Peter Block that : "If leadership is the process of translating intentions into reality- we must be more clear about our intentions. School board policies tend to identify what the board doesn't want in its system. I think I hear Susan saying that she would like to see school board policy identify desired behavior and results. Who has a reaction to that?"

"I do," Michael said. "I like what she said very much. I've always considered policy to be prohibiting rather than empowering. I like empowering better. There's really nothing about prohibiting that draws us toward excellence. I would like our policy and practice to be a two-way street for us and our community to promote the idea that a board such as ours is likely to do things such as that."

"I still don't like policy at all," Ron said, "but I've learned from experience that it's a lot easier to identify what you don't want than what you do want."

"There's no doubt about that," Jerry said, "but we didn't get elected to take the easy way out. I think we should give serious thought to being certain that our policy identifies what we want. I'll admit that when we talk about tying policy and vision together as we seem to be doing now, I'm on the fringe of my knowledge. But, I think I know enough to recognize that If we don't know where we're going, we're not likely to get there. I want to be a member of a board that's proactive."

"I'm a little confused about this issue," Don said. "I attended a session about policy governance at NSBA last year. The presenter was advocating policy manuals which only include behaviors that the board would not put up with. Now, we're talking about exactly the opposite. I'd like to hear your comments about that, Larry."

Larry laughed and looked as if he'd just as soon not have had that question asked. Then he said: "Policy governance focuses on limitations rather than empowerment. It appeals to absentee corporate boards that meet only a couple of times a year. It seems to work for them. Some school boards have decided that policy governance is a good way to deal with school board policy. However, unlike corporate board members, the members of school boards live in the district where the action takes place. They have considerable knowledge about the operation of the school system and interact on a daily basis with both those who are employed by and those who are served by the school district. I believe that most school board members would prefer to take a positive and proactive role in policy development. Generally, school boards want to have more influence on what matters in the school district."

"But doesn't that put the board in danger of attempting to micromanage the school district?" Don asked. "I don't want to be accused of that."

Larry responded, "That's a good question, Don. But I have found just the opposite to be true. By tending to policy, the board can have more influence on what happens in the school district and be less at risk of getting lost in details."

"We've already concluded that far too many board policies are really administrative procedures," Sylvia observed. "Why have school boards allowed this to happen?"

Larry responded, "I've observed that, surprisingly, many of these 'faux policies' are adopted by boards at the request of school administrators. They often address 'hot button' issues where administrators feel the need for visible board support."

"I've thoroughly enjoyed this discussion on policy," he said. "I believe we can do it right. I'd like to see us explore the establishment of a procedure to check on a continuing basis for alignment of our policy with our guidance system."

"You've lost me again," Ron said. "I don't see how policy has anything whatsoever to do with our guidance program. Help me out, Mark."

Mark realized again that the board would have a significant challenge in helping Ron achieve maximum effectiveness. He was determined to do his part. He couldn't afford to give up on Ron. So, he patiently responded, "By guidance system, I mean our vision, values, beliefs and goals. I'm talking about being certain that board policies are consistent with and promote our vision. Beyond that, they need to be aligned with the board's values, beliefs and goals. We need to know that administrative procedures, rules, regulations and practices are all aligned with our policies. To put it simply, what we say in policy and what happens in our school system must be consistent."

"That makes sense," Ron said." Why didn't you just say that in the first place?"

Mark's Reflection.

Mark thought that Larry had done an exceptionally good job of guiding the board through a discussion of policy. He was encouraged by the board's response. He saw the possibility that this board had the potential to do a better job with school board policy than any board he had ever known. He actually felt that this board might learn to use policy to move the board in the direction of its vision and simultaneously enhance the community's confidence in the school board. The board seems to be ready to use its policies for guidance and encouragement rather than control. It's much more likely that policy contributes to the health of the system, if it is not used for control. He was increasingly pleased that he is a member of this board. He would continuously remind himself about the importance of being patient with fellow board members, especially Ron. He would carefully avoid reacting too quickly to negative comments and instead would make a special effort to make certain his comments were "board building" comments.

Questions for discussion

1. How realistic is it to say that policy is the board acting when it is not in session? Why would you endorse or reject the statement?
2. Why is it important to distinguish between administrative procedures and policy? What if the administration wants the board to pass an administrative regulation and call it policy?
3. What are some actions that help to make policy known and understood around the district?
4. What would the board do when its policy manual becomes cumbersome and seldom consulted?
5. What did Sylvia mean when she said, "We will use our policy to give voice to our vision?"
6. Why is it important to have policy aligned with the system's guidance system?

CHAPTER 7

The Retreat: Vision

AS A NEW session began, Larry reminded the Board that "Articulate a Vision" was identified in an earlier session as the first job of the board. He reminded them that the issue of focus on a few issues had also been raised earlier. He said, "Articulating a vision is about verbally painting a picture of what the school district will be like when we get it to where we want it to be." Then, he asked board members if they knew what they wanted the school district to become.

Susan was the first to respond: "Setting a vision of what we want our schools to become should be easy. Doesn't everyone pretty well agree on what we want schools to be?" She continued, "As a mother, I want our school to teach my children what they need to know and be able to do to be successful in school and in life. Is that not what every parent wants schools to do?"

"I don't disagree with you, Susan," Don replied, "but that's an extremely broad statement. It's not exactly a clear picture of what we want our school district to become."

Jerry added, "That's for sure, some of my kids seem to benefit more than others in the same school situation."

Susan and Jerry have spoken of their interest as parents," Michael said. "Perhaps that's where we should begin. Our vision will need to consider the aspirations of parents of the children in our schools."

Larry went to the smartboard and wrote: Visions are detected, not erected.

While Larry was writing and before he could comment, Don interrupted," I hope that you new board members don't think the board was operating without a vision before you were elected. The board gave attention to vision in our policy manual as well as our mission statement and beliefs." Then he added, "Progress County is frequently recognized for having one of the most up-to-date policy manuals in the state. In fact, several school districts have used our policy manual as a model for theirs." Unfortunately, he didn't pass on the opportunity to end his comment with a reminder that he led the process as President of the Board during most of the updating.

A quiet pause in the conversation seemed to indicate that no one intended to respond directly to Don's comment. So Sylvia added, "The real question is not whether we have a vision statement; it's whether our vision statement provides guidance to the board and to our staff and the citizens of the school district. There's a big difference between having a vision statement and operating as a visionary board."

"Perceptive comment," Larry said. "I think Sylvia is challenging us to look at vision as the centerpiece of a guidance system. She's suggesting that our vision is a standard by which we judge whether a proposed action would help us to become what we want to be." Then Larry asked, "Do you think she has given us the real test of effective vision?"

"What she said sounded good," noted Don, "but we continue to get more and more state and federal mandates telling us what we must do. I like the idea of having our own guidance system but I don't understand how we can do that with all of these mandates. Local control is getting to be a thing of the past."

"You raise a valid issue, Don," Sylvia observed. "But even with the overreaching federal and state mandates, there is still some room for choices that we can make to shape a compelling picture of what our school district can become. The question is, are we up to that task?"

"When we signed on to the board, we knew that there would be tough challenges," added Michael. "Just talking about vision is new to most of us. It's a significant challenge for us to lead in the development of a vision and a giant step for us to commit to be guided by that vision. But, if we can learn how to do it together, I have no doubt that it will take us to a new level of effectiveness." Michael paused, smiled and dramatically said, "That's exciting to me."

"It scares me," Jerry confessed, "I'm not much of a vision person. Vision is too fluffy for me. I like something a little more solid. I have to understand how something will work before I can support it."

"I'd like to know more about how it will work too," added Susan. "Michael said earlier that we need to consider what parents in our school district want for their children. I'd like for us to do that, but I have no idea about how we would go about it."

"I don't think the board itself will be able to collect the vision from the community," Mark said. "We'll need help with that, but we can decide how to do that later. What the board needs to do first is to decide if we genuinely want community input and, if so, do we sincerely intend to use it?"

"I agree," Michael said, "The important thing now, is for us to determine that we are going to participate and invite our community to join us in the visioning process."

"We don't need to encourage parents to come to our board meetings to tell us what they want for their children?" Ron objected. "We'll have more parents and more advice than we want without asking. Besides, we have some nuts in our community that we don't want to crack open. The last thing we need is for them to come to a board meeting."

"As Mark said earlier, the board won't collect community input at board meetings. It will do that through organized sessions led by others, Sylvia reminded the board. "But if we want community input and community support, we'll want it from all segments of the community."

"Visualizing is an inclusive process," Larry advised. "It is a team sport and some team members will be better than others, but we still need to let them play. We need to understand before we begin the process that not all suggestions will be useful."

Jerry added, "I'm leaning toward supporting the process of visioning. I like the idea of asking our community what it expects from our school system. Our schools belong to the community, not just to the board. But, I'm wondering if it would be wise to commit to this without knowing exactly how it will work."

In an effort to further ease apprehension, Larry shared a few thoughts from Peter Block's book entitled **The Answer to How Is Yes**. He also called attention to an Abraham Lincoln quote, "Determine that the thing can and shall be done and then we shall find the way."

This appeared to free the board members to explore ideas about the potential outcomes and processes of visioning without feeling the need to fill in all the blanks.

Several board members reacted to the idea of committing to doing something before clearly knowing how to do it. In some of the comments there was reluctance and in others a sense of a new challenge. All members of the board seemed to speak freely and felt comfortable in collectively exploring what it would mean to take the next step.

During the hour of discussion, Larry listed the following related considerations on the smartboard:

- The decision about how we will make our decisions is one of the most important ones we will make.
- A clearly stated intention to effectively use vision releases an awesome power.
- It's a different way to "do business."
- We need honest front-end sharing of the challenge and potential.
- We have little experience with visioning, so we'll likely have some struggles with it as we learn.
- The absence of great examples from other districts is a further challenge and not an insurmountable obstacle.
- Until a commitment is made by the board, nothing significant will happen.
- This is an ongoing process which will be revisited and revised as we learn together.
- One of the early decisions to be made involves the approaches to be taken to harvest the aspirations of the community
- All input will be collected with no ideas rejected or praised at this point.
- This process will result in a sense of ownership and greater support by the community.

The discussion was lively and comments from board members indicated a wide range of viewpoints, some doubt but most reflecting a positive expectancy.

Jerry recalled that Sylvia had said that the board talked and talked but did nothing, it would have failed the children and people who voted for them. He asked, "How can we be certain that this whole process is not an exercise in talking rather than doing?"

Lindell, who had remained mostly an observer, responded, "The administrative staff takes the collected vision and uses it to guide the development of a strategic plan. The plan includes annual and long term goals for the school district to be considered for adoption by the board. When we don't have to include a number of 'pet projects' we can focus on a smaller number of goals. The fewer goals we have in our plan, the more likely we are to achieve them."

Jerry thanked Lindell and said that his explanation made perfect sense to him.

Larry began to wrap up the session by commending the board for outstanding participation during the session. He said the conversation about vision had been excellent. He encouraged the board to ask Lindell to take what he has heard in this discussion and begin to develop a plan for the board's consideration, setting out steps to articulate and move toward operating from a clear and compelling vision.

Sylvia thanked Larry for his leadership of the session and also commended her fellow board members for their openness and honesty during the session. She observed, "Some of us have stated that we sought positions on this Board with the prospect that we could help the district to solve some of our problems. Changing our style to work toward our vision will largely leave the problem solving to our administrators. This change will both help to prevent problems before they arise and provide a guidance system for employees to use to handle problems that do arise." She added, "This is a challenge that I'm confident our board can meet."

"I agree, said Michael, "I hope that we're ready to make the commitment."

A sense of accomplishment was evident as the members wrapped up this session. Board members were beginning to realize that articulating a vision could provide inspiration, guidance, and support. A clear and compelling vision can be a recruiting tool to invite the community to be a partner to the effort. They also were more clear in their understanding that visioning as a way of life empowers a board to create "what we want to become."

Mark's Reflection

Mark could hardly believe that the board had participated in what he thought was a "remarkable session." He would not have thought that all members of the board were at all receptive to the notion of visioning. He knew that a lot more work would be required if they were to become a board using vision as a guidance system. But, they would now have a plan being developed by Lindell and his staff to consider. Mark was thrilled to think how the board would be fulfilling its community leadership function by engaging the community in visioning. He believed that both the effectiveness of the board would be increased and the public image and support of the board would be enhanced.

He judged that he could contribute to the process by asking himself and his colleagues a different kind of question as they oversee the school district. This thought reminded him of one of his favorite statements: "Our knowledge is demonstrated by the answers we give and our wisdom by the questions we ask." He sensed that sessions like this were helping board members to become wiser by asking better questions. He realized that collective visioning tended to be more effective when individuals experienced some of it in their personal lives. At least for now, he was proud of his board.

He thought that board members were becoming more comfortable with and trusting of each other. Jerry's comment about vision being fluffy and not solid enough for him was not adequately answered; we need to help him with that issue before it arises at a critical time. One thing Mark had learned was that the time to evaluate a policy or practice was when there was no enforcement in the pipeline. He thought it helped that members of the board were becoming more willing to ignore rather than challenge comments such as those made by Don attempting to give himself credit for his leadership of the board. He reminded himself that he could help the board grow in its ability to challenge what should be challenged and leave unchallenged things that would not help to build board unity or were not worth the time and effort to challenge.

Questions for discussion

1. **Why might a board sometimes find it helpful to commit to do something without having a clear sense of how it should be done?**
2. **Why might a vision statement sometimes be a bit fuzzy around the edges but crystal clear at the center?**
3. **How should the board's vision impact policy making and budgeting?**
4. **How important is an articulated vision to board effectiveness?**
5. **How might members having articulated their personal vision give impact to the visioning of the board?**
6. **What is the implication of Sylvia's statement: "The real question is not whether we have a vision statement; it's whether our vision statement provides guidance to the board and to our staff and the citizens of the school district?"**

CHAPTER 8

Community Leadership

LARRY BEGAN THE next session of the retreat by asking board members if they considered community leadership as one of the major functions of the school board. The puzzled look on their faces suggested that they had no idea what he was talking about. He suggested to them that in his opinion it was one of the three most important responsibilities of a school board. He called their attention to the words that Sylvia had written on the smart board: We must enhance the credibility of this board.

He reminded the board that elected officials generally were not held in high esteem throughout our country today. He said that public confidence in both state legislatures and Congress is incredibly low. He suggested that the public's lack of confidence in state and federal lawmakers had adversely affected public confidence in local school boards, which he thought was higher than that of lawmakers but nowhere near as high as it should be. He asked if members of the board agreed or disagreed with that observation.

"I don't really care what the public thinks about me," Ron said. "I'm on the school board to help the children, not the public. Although, I sometimes get compliments from the public for some of the things I say and the questions I ask."

"You and I obviously run in different circles," Susan said." As I was campaigning, an overwhelming majority of the people who talked with me about the school board viewed the board in a negative light. Some expressed high regard for an individual member of the board but I can't recall a single person who expressed high regard for the board as a whole."

"Please don't take my remarks as personal," Jerry said, "but when I was campaigning for the school board, it was fairly obvious that several people weren't as enthusiastic about voting for me nearly as much as they were to vote against my opponent who, of course, was a member of this board." He continued, "People frequently expressed a desire for the entire board to be voted out of office. None of us would want to be identified with a group characterized in the way that this board seemed to be regarded by a significant number of citizens of our community."

"When I was president of the board,"Don said, "I did everything I knew to do to enhance the reputation of this board. I tried to honor people at board meetings and I consistently made public comments about what a pleasure it was to serve with the members of this board in trying to provide better educational opportunities for children. I intended for my comments to cause the public to be more supportive of the board."

"I guess we have to conclude that your strategy didn't work," Sylvia said. "I'll bet that if we conducted a survey, at least 75% of the people in our county would rate their confidence level in the school board as low."

Larry interrupted the discussion to suggest that the issue of public confidence in the school board is at least a concern to most members. Of course, it is important to notice that as people have more decisions made somewhere else by someone else, they tend to exercise the ones that are left and voting out is more noticeable than continuing. He asked Ron if he would be willing to go along with the "more sensitive" board members in considering ways to enhance the public confidence in the board. Ron seemed to relish the attention. "I'd do almost anything for this board," he said, "even though I think there are more important things we could be doing with our time instead of worrying about what the community thinks of the board."

"Let's explore the board's responsibility for community leadership and consider how exercising this responsibility might lead to a more effective board and, in turn, result in enhanced public confidence in the board," Larry suggested.

"I'll be the first one on board that train," Susan said enthusiastically." Let's get it rolling."

Larry asked, "What comes to your mind when you think of community leadership?"

"I think about my time in the Army," Ron said. "I was a Master Sergeant and had responsibilities to lead a group of men. The first thing I had to know is where I was leading them or what I was leading them to do. In this case, I suppose we're going to lead the community to accomplish something or go somewhere."

Larry thanked him for his insight. "That's a good start. To where does the board want to lead the community or what does it want to lead the community to do? I added to where to go the matter of what to do. A few years ago leadership consultants suggested that the best way to get people to join an effort was to be very clear about where we were going. That's a luxury that we no longer have ; now we are being told to make sure that "the right people are on the bus before deciding where we are going. This concept emphasizes inclusion as well as direction."

"We want to lead the members of our community to get involved with the schools," said Jerry. "Hopefully, their involvement will lead to support and support will mean better funding and better funding will mean better schools."

"Do we want to lead them to become involved or do we want to lead them to become engaged?" Mark asked.

"Is there a difference?" Jerry asked.

"I think there's a major difference," Mark responded. "It's like the difference between owning a business or being a patron of the business. I think we want our community to feel that they own the schools and the board should treat them like owners. Involvement can be something we do to others; engagement is always the decision of the person to connect with something of interest or value."

"I'd appreciate it if you'd develop that idea a little bit more," Susan said. "I'm not yet able to see the distinction clearly."

Mark responded, "Let's suppose we all went to a deli for a sandwich at the same time and found that there were already several customers waiting to be served. As a patron, we'd probably go somewhere else to eat. As an owner, we might jump behind the counter, grab an apron and gloves and start making sandwiches or maybe serving as cashier. In the process, we'd make cheerful and encouraging remarks and do what we could to handle the crowd efficiently and keep them in the sandwich shop until they could be served." Mark continued, "We want the citizens of our community to feel ownership of the schools and do whatever they can to make them effective rather than criticizing our schools or even taking their children somewhere else for their schooling."

Susan thanked him and even said that he'd provided an excellent story which clarified the issue for her. Larry also thanked him and other members of the board nodded in agreement.

Larry wrote on the smartboard:

Engage the community as OWNERS of the schools

He challenged the members of the board to identify ways the board needed to exercise community leadership in order to improve the effectiveness of the board while enhancing the community's confidence in the board.

Don was the first to respond." I think that if our community understood the issues before the board and how this board makes decisions, it would be far more supportive of the board. I think members of the board consistently vote to do what we think is right."

In a bit of an unusual move, Sylvia agreed with Don." There's no question about it, the better the community understands the issues the board faces, the more likely it is to support the actions of the board as long as it appears to be the right action. That's why I think the board has to pay more attention to being certain that the community understands our actions. We have to be willing to talk to Margie and explain the board's thinking. Sometimes that will mean that we have to spend some time as a board reflecting on our actions. Experience is not the best teacher. We learn not from experience but from reflecting on the experience."

"She may be right," Michael suggested. "It has never occurred to me that the board should spend time reflecting on what it learned from an experience. I can see how that might increase the level of wisdom that goes into some of our board policies and how the board would benefit from the experience and the community might understand the board action better. It's not a stretch to think that the community's perception of the board could be enhanced significantly by that process."

Not all board members were persuaded by the arguments. "Sounds like a major waste of time to me," Ron grumbled. "I don't want to take more time to decide why the board made the decision it made. It should be fairly obvious to anyone who cares. Making a decision is hard enough but trying to figure out why we made it just doubles the work."

"I don't see much benefit in taking time to discuss why we made a decision, Don said. "We have a hard enough time getting through our agenda as it is. When I was board chairman, I had to push hard to keep everyone on track so we could get our business finished at a reasonable hour."

"If I understand correctly, it's not just why we made the decision as much as it is to reflect on what we learned from how we handled the issue," Jerry said,"

"I like the idea,"Michael said, "but I'm not exactly sure how it should work. As Board President, am I supposed to suggest that before we move on to the next item on the agenda that we stop to reflect upon what we learned from our action on the previous item?"

"I don't think that's necessary for most items," Mark said, "But I would consider it to be very appropriate and worthwhile to occasionally do that for major items soon after the board has dealt with them. As we begin to practice reflection, we will find at least 3 kinds to consider: hindsight reflection looks back at our decision or action; foresight reflection allows us to anticipate the consequences before we live them; insight reflection asks us to look at the learning in which the decision or action is embedded."

"Like what? Could you give us an illustration?" Jerry asked.

"For example, if the board terminated a tenured teacher," Mark explained, "I should think there would be some things that we would learn from the process. We know that some people would likely be upset with the teacher's dismissal. If we take time to reflect on the situation and identify a few of the things we learned, at least two things are accomplished. First, there may be some policy issues that would be clarified. Second, we'll be better prepared individually to share the board's position with the community."

Mark continued, "We don't take actions arbitrarily. We take action based upon the facts. If we reach a conclusion based on the facts, isn't it logical that community members who understand the situation will arrive at the same conclusion as we did. I'm confident that the more the community understands the issue, the more it will support our action."

Susan added: "As I thought, or maybe, reflected on our last few observations, it seems that if we look at the challenge of getting through the agenda and add insight reflection we might see that our purpose was not just to get through but, to do important things." There was a sense of agreement and appreciation for Susan's willingness to try some of the things we are focusing on.

Larry wrote on the smartboard:

**Reflect on major decisions and
share learnings with the community**

"What is another way the board can exercise community leadership to improve the effectiveness of the board and enhance the community's confidence in the board?" Larry asked.

"We have a lot of wonderful things happening in our schools," Sylvia observed." We need to do a better job of sharing those success stories with our community. As owners of the schools, the members of the community will surely want to hear stories about their success. I love to hear stories about good things my children have done. And I like the people more who tell me those stories. Don't you think that our community wants to hear success stories about their schools? Don't you think success stories would help build support for our schools and enhance the credibility of our school board at the same time?"

Larry was smiling from ear to ear. "I don't know if I've ever partici-pated in a better retreat," he said. "If you believe the answer to each of' Sylvia's questions is 'yes,' raise your hand. Everyone in the room raised a hand except Margie. She raised both hands and said, "Let me help you tell the stories. Please let me help you tell them!"

"I love the idea," Michael said, "but we have to find some way to be intentional about doing this. I'm not sure how we'll get the stories or how we'll tell them. What do you think about this idea, Lindell?"

"I think it's a wonderful idea," Lindell said, "I can think of several ways off the top of my head. I'd be happy to draft a policy to implement this and bring it to the next board meeting for your consideration."

"That would be wonderful," said Michael "Would you share a couple right now?"

"Sure," Lindell said, "I'll present the core of a couple of undeveloped ideas.

First, I could invite each principal to share at least one success story with me each month. Our staff could select one or two for presenta-tion to the board at each meeting if you wanted to make that a short feature at each meeting.

Second, we could sponsor a writing competition and ask our students to write stories about how a school employee has made a difference in their lives. We could either select one or two of these to be presented at a school board meeting or we could possibly start a feature in the local newspaper if we could get Margie to give us some advice about how to do that and how to publish the stories."

Lindell advised, "That's just a couple of ideas off the top of my head. My staff will have more. We could develop a few proposals like these if you'd like us to and present them for your consideration at the next board meeting."

"If those are undeveloped ideas off the top of your head, I'm anxious to see what they look like when you've had time to consider them further," Susan said. "I'm excited about the possibilities."

"What do you think, Margie?" Michael asked." Is this a good idea?"

"It is not a good idea." Margie said,"It's a great idea! I have no doubt that the board will be thrilled with the result," Margie responded confidently."

Larry might not have described it in quite as glowing terms but he was highly impressed with the idea. He wrote on the smart board:

Share Success Stories with the Community

He turned to the board and said, "I love it!" Then, he called for an idea about another way the board can exercise community leadership to improve the effectiveness of the board and enhance the community's confidence in the board.

"Before we leave the idea of sharing success stories with the community," Sylvia interrupted, "I'm thinking that I'd love to have some of these stories that I could share with people in the community as I talk with them. It strikes me that personally sharing success stories can be an effective way for each of us to exercise community leadership."

Larry commended Sylvia for her suggestion and said that he highly recommended such action. Then, he again asked for other ways the board could exercise community leadership.

"I don't know whether this complements or is a part of the previous item" Michael said, "I think an important part of community leadership is the recognition and celebration of the accomplishment of our students and our staff."

"I think that's important too," Sylvia said. "School employees need to know that the board recognizes and appreciates what they do for our students. Every day, we have employees who go above and beyond the call of duty and receive little or no recognition for it. It seems to me that we've abrogated our responsibilities when we fail to recognize the achievements of our staff. The same is certainly true with our students. As far as whether this comes under the previous item – sharing success stories, I think that sharing success stories and celebrating achievements are two different things. We need to recognize and celebrate success."

"I think that they are related," Don said, "but we can share success stories without celebrating and we could celebrate without sharing success stories. There's not much chance we're going to overdo it, so let's list them as separate items."

Larry walked to the smart board and wrote:

Recognize and Celebrate Success

Before Larry could ask for the next suggestion, Michael spoke up.

"This may fall under the first item you have on the smart board, but I think we need a way to hear from our community about its expectations for our schools--not just one time-- but on a continuing basis. If we want community support, we need to know what the citizens of our community are expecting of their schools. That is part of engagement but I suspect the community could be engaged without us necessarily having a process for hearing from the community. Does that make sense?"

"It makes sense to me," Susan said." Before I was on the board, I had ideas that I would like to have shared with the board but I didn't think I should take up the time of the board by asking to be on the agenda. I just wanted to share an idea for the board's consideration."

"Lindell, It would be very helpful if you would have the staff consider ways the board can glean ideas from the public on a continuing basis. I'm also going to ask each member of the board to consider ideas for getting feedback from the community so that we can be prepared to discuss this when we hear back from the staff," Michael said.

Lindell agreed to work with the staff in brainstorming and drafting ideas for getting feedback from the community on a continuing basis. " We're very likely to include one-on-one communication for each of you board members with your constituents," he said. "I suspect that each board member should feel some responsibility to share what the board is doing with the community and to glean from the community what it expects of the board and our school system. That certainly won't be the only strategy that we will propose but I suspect it will be one that we'll propose."

"I can tell you right now," Ron said, "I have learned from experience. When we start asking the public what they think we are inviting a pot full of complaints. We'll get so many complaints we won't know what to do with them."

"Ron, I hope you learned from our earlier conversation that experience is not the best teacher," Susan kidded. "May I suggest that you reflect on your experience and be prepared to share what you've learned with us when we discuss it at our school board meeting."

"I'm not much of a reflector, "Ron responded. "I try to be a light, not a reflector, but I'll make an exception since you asked so nicely."

Larry reminded the group that the agenda for the retreat included a session on vision. He said that it will relate closely to this discussion. Then he wrote on the smartboard:

**Establish and maintain an ongoing process for
seeking and using ideas or recommendations from
the community to improve public schools**

Then, he called for another way the board can exercise community leadership to improve the effectiveness of the board and enhance the community's confidence in the board.

"I'm thinking about what Ron said earlier," Susan said. "He said if we ask for community input we get a lot of complaints. Although we should consider being a reflector, I think he shed some light on the situation for me. I want to be certain that we aren't inviting wholesale complaints. So, I wonder if we could adopt a standard operating procedure that when we receive complaints, we listen to them and then ask the person bringing the complaint to restate it in a way that shows their commitment to a better way of doing things?"

"If I understand your suggestion," Michael said, "I like it. Are you suggesting that we receive no complaints simply as complaints? And, in order for the board to consider what might have been intended as a complaint, the person bringing it must restate it as a suggestion for improvement?"

"Yes, that's what I'm suggesting," Susan replied. "I know that we need to use good judgment in the way we do this. I'm asking the board to help me think it through and modify it as needed. We don't want anyone to misunderstand our intentions. What we want to do is to get all the members of our community to accept the responsibility to help make our schools better. So, instead of submitting a complaint we ask them to turn it into a suggestion for improvement. They may choose to support their suggestion with facts about how our system has failed, but every complaint is accompanied by a proposal for improvement."

"That's a novel idea, but I like novel ideas," Jerry said." What's your opinion of this, Larry? Do you think it will work?"

Larry didn't respond verbally. He walked to the board and wrote:

Turn Complaints into Suggestions for Making the
School System Better

"There's my answer," he said. "I have never heard of any school board doing anything like this. What a powerful and different approach. We're on a roll. Let's keep it going."

Sylvia said, "Maybe this is the most obvious one of all. Let's make our school board meetings be windows for the community. And, let's be sure that when the community looks through those windows they see board members demonstrating exemplary conduct, diligently working for the benefit of children, treating each other as well as those appearing before our board with respect and consistently showing by the decisions we make that we are champions for children."

"That might require the biggest change of all," Michael said." I don't believe we've done that very well. But when we do that, I don't have the slightest doubt that our community will respond by supporting and showing great confidence in our board. We can do this, can't we?"

Larry walked to the smart board and wrote:

Make Board Meetings Windows
Through Which the Community Sees Excellence

"Is that acceptable to everyone?" he asked.

Every member nodded or said, "Yes, we do."

Larry asked, "Is there any other way the board can exercise community leadership to improve the effectiveness of the board and enhance the community's confidence in the board?"

Mark reminded the board that it depended upon the County Commission for funding the local portion of the school budget. He said that school boards and county commissions frequently seemed to have less than exemplary relationships. He characterized such a relationship as harmful to adequate funding for schools. He suggested that improving the relationship with the County Commission is a function of community leadership.

Sylvia suggested, "We can make major strides in improving the board's relationship to the county commission but we need to develop a strategy for doing so. To begin with, we need to stop calling them unfavorable names and stop using derogatory terms to describe them."

"I have been embarrassed about our relationship with the County Commission," Michael said." It doesn't take a mental giant to recognize that our schools are not going to be funded as well as they could be when there's no trust between the board and County Commission. We can and must improve our relationship with them."

"I've never cared much for our County Commission," Ron said. "Most of its members don't want to fund schools. They don't want to pay any taxes nor do anything progressive. They wouldn't raise taxes if we all struck oil. It's hard for me to respect people like that and I'm not going to be two-faced about it."

On a lighter note, Mark said, "Ron, all we need you to do is to be light. You said that you try to be light. Just help them see that better schools benefit our community and that a better relationship with the board benefits us all. Can you do that?"

Ron grinned and said, "You got me on that one. I guess I don't have much of a choice, do I?"

Larry walked to the smart board and wrote.

Establish a Partnership with the Funding Body

Sylvia said, "I can't let us leave this topic without talking about the board's responsibility for dealing with the media. That certainly seems to me to be an Important part of community leadership. We have a positive relationship with the media and I think most of us get along well with Margie but we aren't taking full advantage of the great resource the media offers us. I'd like to see us explore strategies for dealing more effectively with the media."

"I never talk to the media and don't ever intend to talk to them in the future," Ron said. "They only take one sentence of what I say and they seem to take the worst one I make. It seems to me that they always try to make me look like a fool."

Mark was thinking that the media didn't need much help with that job but he only thought about it. In fact, he wasn't the only one thinking it, but the board moved on and no one said it.

"I have a question for you Larry," Susan said." As a new school board member I need some hints about working with the media. Tell us who should speak to the media on behalf of the board?"

Larry started to speak but before he could answer, Don interrupted," When I was Board President I felt that it was my responsibility to speak for the board."

"So, now that you're not Board President, you feel an obligation to speak for me and answer a question that I'm asked?" Larry joked. Then he said, "I see it very differently. No one speaks for the board until the board has spoken. If the board has spoken, then each member of the board has an obligation to speak for the board and support the board action. That is an important part of community leadership."

"I was talking about speaking for the board in reacting to public opinion," Don said."

"A good board doesn't react to public opinion," Larry replied." It creates it."

"Wow! That's powerful stuff. I will need to think about that some more," Sylvia said."I'm beginning to see why you said the board can use community leadership to both improve the effectiveness of the board and enhance the community's confidence in the board."

"While we're on the subject," Mark said,"It occurs to me that as individual members of the board we need to exercise some caution in attempting to create public opinion before the board has spoken. When Margie calls me to ask my opinion on a matter on the agenda for our next meeting, if I share my opinion with her and she prints it in the newspaper, I have gone public with my position and I am likely to defend my position rather than be open to opposing opinions. By going public with my opinion, I've made it much more difficult to be open minded and perhaps to change my mind once I've heard the thinking of the superintendent and my fellow board members. I think it might be better if I tell Margie that I'm weighing the issue carefully and that I look forward to the discussion at the board meeting where I will hear the recommendation of the superintendent and the opinions of my fellow board members before I finalize my position. It seems that to do otherwise is a bit disrespectful of our superintendent, the rest of the board and anyone who might appear before the board to speak on the issue."

"Exactly," Larry said. "Seldom will you find a public official who understands that. But, I could not agree with you more. You owe it to each other to listen to and respect the opinions of fellow board members and your superintendent. The decisions your board makes will be better when you don't paint yourself into a corner by taking a position before you've allowed for the development of the collective wisdom of the board and other members of the leadership team.

I had not thought of it that way before," Michael observed," but it makes sense. It is much more difficult for the board to reach consensus or even have an enlightened discussion when members have taken a public position on the issue."

Susan added, "Before we start discussing an issue that comes before the board there are probably as many different opinions as there are members of the board. When we go public with our positions before the board meets, we are in essence leading our community to be pulled in seven different directions. If we are to be effective in community leadership, we need to lead in a single direction."

Susan added, "We have to reach a single decision and although we hopefully will be able to do that following our board discussion, the members of our community who do not attend the board meeting will still be divided. They won't have the benefit of our discussion and they won't come together behind our decision."

"I don't think we have a responsibility to lead our community in any direction," Ron said." I'm here to vote for what I think is best for the kids. It seems pretty simple to me. I don't care much what the community thinks."

Mark smiled. He was pleased to observe that the board was already learning that every remark by a board member did not deserve a response. This was sure to make board meetings more civil and help the board appear more professional in the eyes of the community.

Without objection, I'm going to add the following to our list," Larry said. He wrote on the smartboard:

Revise Policy on Working with the Media

Larry closed out the session by briefly recapping each point he had written on the smartboard. He commended the members for excellent participation and said he was excited about what this board could achieve when members recognize and accept their responsibility for community leadership.

Mark's Reflection

Mark was excited too. He had thoroughly enjoyed this session and he believed that the board had already become a better board. But, he could hardly wait to spend more time reflecting on this session and further developing ideas about the potential and power of community leadership. One of the things becoming more clear to Mark was the likely disconnect between what we know and how we act. He knew that people do not change their minds nor their positions because they have been presented with new facts and information. We change our minds from stories that we choose to tell ourselves and others. He believed that and yet had never seen so clearly the importance of creating new stories that reflect our vision. The complaint- to- suggestion approach is consistent with an idea that ,perhaps, we complain in part because we have a vision of a better way to operate. There is so much more value in identifying that part of our vision that is not being realized. He had not fully realized how much he would enjoy reaction with board members at this retreat.

Questions for Discussion

1. How might our desire to involve everyone interfere with a more desirable level of engaging our citizens? What's the difference?
2. What are some simple, but effective, ways to get success stories into the public awareness?
3. What changes does your board need to make to have your meetings become windows through which the Community Sees Excellence?
4. How does recognizing and sharing success build community support for the schools and the board?
5. How seriously does your board consider its community leadership role?
6. Which part of the board's community leadership role appeals to you most?

CHAPTER 9

Lindell's Retirement Announcement

SUPERINTENDENT LINDELL SHARP shared with the School Board early in the academic year his intention to retire at the end of the year. "Today I'm announcing my plans to retire on December 31 of this year. I have been honored to serve this board and our school system through a period of dynamic change during the past ten years. Many of the changes mandated by State and Federal directives have required us to go about our work in very different ways than those I have long supported. We are not where we want to be as a system, and yet I am pleased with the progress we have made. I leave you with a dedicated and passionate staff that not only stimulates and engages our students academically but also works to provide a safe and nurturing environment where students can gain the social and emotional skills that they will need to be successful in life. I'm announcing my retirement now in order to allow the board adequate time to find a qualified superintendent to succeed me. You will have any assistance from me that you want during this process."

Several board members expressed their appreciation for Lindell and the leadership he had provided for the system. Ron thanked him for the years which they had shared. "I will miss you," observed Michael, and "I appreciate your notice of retirement allowing us enough time to do a thorough job of finding a replacement to continue our progress. I warn you that I intend to do everything I can to make these last few months both the most productive and rewarding time of your career."

Don added his appreciation and noted that "Our School Board has many important tasks and none is more important than that of selecting a Superintendent to lead our school system with the professionalism and insight that Lindell has shown. No one has more influence on everything that happens in the system. As much effort as we might make, we won't be an effective school board unless we choose a solid, strong and capable superintendent."

As the members reflected on Lindell's retirement, they became more aware that the 'understandings' between the board and its superintendent of ten years would not automatically transfer to a new relationship.

"We now have the opportunity and necessity of clarifying our guidance system as it relates to this Board and its new Superintendent," noted Mark. Other members expressed a similar view and yet they were coming to realize that a lot of work will be required if we are to fully capitalize on this opportunity.

Sylvia noted that "We will probably want to seek some guidance from Larry and we'll all surely want to attend a session on Superintendent Selection at the NSBA Convention."

The retirement news was received with an evolving appreciation for the fact that the relationship with Lindell- though sometimes strained- was never hostile and the Board could expect cooperation from the superintendent in the all-important task of finding the best possible chief executive officer.

"I think that we have some well-qualified people working in our system now," observed Ron. "Surely we can pick one of them to be Lindell's successor. That would save us a lot of time and money and let our administrators know that we have confidence in them."

Ron's idea garnered some additional support until Sylvia shared her view on the subject. "Ron is correct in saying that we have qualified people in the system and, perhaps we will eventually select one of them to be superintendent. I have listened to other board members at conferences as they've told of their experience in selecting a superintendent. They shared ways in which their systems were made better as their boards clarified their board-superintendent relationship. I would like our board to do something like that as we face the reality of Lindell's retirement."

Other board members quickly added their reaction and a consensus emerged that the board would use the replacement process as a time to review the leadership team and clarify expectations.

Susan spoke what others were thinking when she expressed the view that "local candidates should be included with others, but the Board should seek the best possible person without regard to where that person has previously worked."

"To help us find the best possible person, we will likely need to secure the services of a search agency or individual," volunteered Michael. "We do not have the time nor the expertise to do that job by ourselves, do we?"

After a few more reactions from members including Ron's expression of confidence in the board's ability to handle the process without assistance, the Board agreed to set a work session to develop a plan for the search. Michael asked Lindell to prepare a plan with the steps involved in the process, possible sources of assistance with the search, and a timeline to allow adequate attention to each step.

Mark's Reflection

As Mark reviewed the discussion and pondered on the situation, he concluded that the selection of our next superintendent is a great time to implement some of the things that we have identified in our retreat. The staff of the system and the community will be extremely interested in the high visibility processes involved in choosing a new superintendent. The odds are that differences around choosing our leader will be rather strong. If we are to build confidence within our community we must go beyond "whom did we choose" to consider "how did we choose." The consideration of candidates within the system is the first topic that came up with our board and it will also be a heavy community concern. The popular view that experience within the system is a big plus will be strong. How can we call attention to the fact that all of our staff has experience within the system without appearing to under appreciate our own? We must find ways to build trust and confidence rather than damaging these important factors. Transparency and accountability will be crucial.

Questions for Discussion

1. What role, if any, should the board ask a retiring superintendent to play in the recruitment or selection of a new superintendent?
2. What is an appropriate response by a board to the retirement of a dedicated and competent superintendent?
3. When an outgoing superintendent retires in the community would it be better for future involvement to depend on personal relationships or be more formal as in a designated "Superintendent Emeritus?"
4. Don said, "We won't be an effective school board unless we choose a solid, strong and capable superintendent." Why do you agree or disagree with his statement?
5. What advantages do you see in the board using the time

immediately after the superintendent's resignation to clarify expectations of their board-superintendent relationship?
6. How constructive is it to identify the former superintendent with
decisions or practices that have fallen into disfavor?

1.

CHAPTER 10

An Open Discussion For New Board Members

MICHAEL FELT THAT the orientation he had when he was a newly elected school board member was woefully inadequate. He had so many questions he wanted to ask at the beginning of his service on the board, but new members were only provided a three hour orientation and almost the entire time was taken up by staff presentations.

He had learned a lot about the school system but not much about being a school board member. He was determined that would not happen to new members under his watch. That's why he scheduled the board retreat early on and why he had now scheduled a session exclusively for new board members to ask questions for discussion by the entire board.

After the obligatory welcome and statement of purpose for the meeting, Michael opened the floor for new members to ask questions. He told board members this was an "open dialogue" and that everyone should feel free to speak at any time so long as someone else was not speaking.

"How do I continue my role as a parent in my school without appearing to exert the power of a school board member?" Susan asked.

Sylvia volunteered to respond: "I tried having my husband handle all issues with our children but I still wanted to be involved in helping out at school projects so I just made certain that I didn't ask for special privileges for my children. It hasn't been a problem at all." She added, "The problems come when school board members abuse their power and seek special treatment."

"Are school board members supposed to visit schools, especially the ones in their district?" Jerry asked.

Michael chose to answer, "I think school board members should visit the schools. It's important that each of us remember that we are not a district superintendent in charge of the schools in our district. I only visit as a goodwill ambassador for the board. I look for things to compliment and I only compliment things that are deserving of a sincere compliment. I want to know how things are going in the schools and I'm often told by staff members that they appreciate my visits but I suspect that is because I'm consistently positive in the remarks that I make. If I encounter something that needs attention, I call it to Lindell's attention and let him handle it without any suggestions from me. I have no authority over the school. It's not the job of a school board member to solve problems in the schools. I try to remember, It's not the job of the school board to run the schools; rather, to see that the schools are run well."

"When you visit a school, do you take a notepad to write down what you observe?" Jerry inquired as a followed up to his previous question.

"Absolutely not." Michael responded. Then he said, "It sends the wrong message and gives the wrong impression for a school board to be writing down things that he or she has observed or requests that have been made. If there is something that is important enough to write down, wait until you get back in your car, then write it down."

How should I handle it when someone complains about something during a visit to a school? Jerry asked.

Don responded, "I listen to them politely since I realize that many people think the school board is the complaint department. Then, I tell the complainer that we have a chain of command that must be followed in solving problems. I remind them that administrators are paid to handle such issues and that if we don't let them handle problems, we never know how well they do it. I tell the person that if I get involved in solving a problem before it reaches the board, I'll be obligated to recuse myself from voting at the board meeting." He added, "That has consistently worked well for me"

"Wow," Ron said. "I wish I had heard that before now. That's a really good idea. I'm going to try that myself."

"I'd like to offer an additional suggestion based upon something that I have recently learned that I believe holds great potential for dealing with complaints." Sylvia added. "I think that as board members, we should challenge the complainer to consider a change that would have prevented such a problem. And, we should suggest that, instead of merely complaining to the appropriate administrator, a more productive approach would be to help the school system be better by proposing an improvement in procedures that would prevent such a problem from occurring in the future.

Mark added, "Complaints can serve a useful purpose. They help us identify policies or practices that at least someone in our educational community believes is not working. They can help us envision a better way of doing things. I like Sylvia's suggestion of encouraging the complainer to help us find a better way. When we do that, we're treating community members like one of the owners of our schools.

Jerry asked, **"What can I say when someone corners me after church to complain about her son's teacher?**

Don asked if he could respond. Then, he said, "Many parents don't know how the school system works or understand the 'chain of command.' However, more commonly, most know it very well, but want to use you to short circuit the process. When a parent approaches you with a complaint about a child's teacher, explain that school board members don't have authority to deal with personnel problems. Ask, 'Have you talked to the teacher?' Suggest that if the conference with the teacher isn't satisfactory, the next step is a conference with the principal and, if necessary, a meeting with the superintendent would be the next step."

"What should a school board member do when a friend asks for a recommendation for a job in the school system?" Susan inquired.

"I'll tell you how I handle it," Sylvia responded with a chuckle. "If I know the person well, I tell them that they may list me as a reference but I don't write letters of recommendation to the school system. I think to do so puts pressure on whoever is making the decision to hire whomever I am recommending. I remind them that any school administrator who is considering their application will check references. That administrator will know me and if I have not written a letter of reference, will likely contact me to ask specific questions. When my opinion is sought and I am asked targeted questions, I will give my honest opinion. However, I believe that as a board we very much want the applicant best qualified for the position to be employed. It's not who they know but what they can do that should count most."

"I'm sure that Sylvia has in mind the best interest of the system and her friend when she agrees to serve as a reference for a prospective employee," added Mark. "I would raise with her and all of you another perspective on the situation. When the system representative who evaluates the applicants notes that one of them has named as a reference a member of the board, is there a tendency to wonder why this tactic is used rather than the listing of another competent person?"

"That is a good point," Sylvia responded. "Perhaps I shouldn't agree to be a reference for people that I know. I've felt that I owed it to both the person and the school system to share the truth about what I know about a person who is seeking employment in the school system. I have, on occasion, recommended that some applicants who have used me as a reference not be hired. I have never felt obligated to recommend someone simply because I was listed as a reference. I'll give that more thought."

"So will I," Susan said. "Both of you have contributed ideas that I can now explore in finding an answer to my own question."

Susan asked, **"How can a school board member help to get money in the budget for things that teachers need?"** She added, "They shouldn't have to buy school supplies out of their own pockets."

Michael responded: "The school board adopts the budget. That gives every member an opportunity to identify areas where funds should be allocated or even to champion a cause. However, any allocation of funds will require a majority vote of the school board. Members have an opportunity to influence the budget through the planning process as goals and objectives are developed and again in the budget process."

Susan asked, **"Can an individual school board member ask the school board attorney for a legal opinion or for legal advice regarding a school issue?"**

Michael responded, "No. Not directly. Bob Lawson has been our school board attorney for fourteen years. He is very knowledgeable about school law and he can answer most questions off the top of his head. Some questions require legal research. Either way, he is paid a retainer and, on top of that, we are billed for his time. Our policy allows for Lindell, the board chair or the board as a whole to request legal opinions. So, you may bring your questions to Lindell or me or you may request an opinion by board action. This protects us, as well as Bob, from excessive requests by individual members as we have experienced in the not-too-distant past."

Don pointed out that the board had adopted a policy that required the superintendent to include in his weekly written reports to the board any requests received from a board member for a legal opinion. He said that he had suggested that policy to avoid individual board members putting pressure on the superintendent and to make the entire board aware of legal issues of importance to any board member. He concluded his remarks with, "That's just one example of the exceptional policies of Progress County."

Sylvia added, "I have been greatly surprised at how little the work of the board is dependent upon legal opinions. I've found that the law is a floor that limits how low we can go; it is not a standard of ethical or moral conduct. When the board is committed to doing the right thing we consistently operate above the law."

What about asking individual staff members, like department directors, to do research on questions we might have about their department, statistics for example?" Susan asked as a follow-up to her previous question.

"The answer is basically the same," Michael responded. "Except we all need to take such requests through the superintendent. We aren't billed for the research our employees do, but they each have full time jobs. We have to protect them from ourselves as individuals.

If the board as a whole protects the staff from board members as individuals,Some board members have an amazing number of questions. Of course, the board as a whole, may request information that requires research."

When can I discuss something with another board member outside a school board meeting? Jerry asked.

Sylvia said, "The easiest way I've heard it explained is this: You can discuss issues with other board members as long as you do not deliberate toward a decision. You may not discuss how you will vote or strategies for gaining support or opposition for issues that will come before the board."

Mark's Reflection

Mark saw value in having an opportunity for new board members to ask questions rather early in their experience on the board. He was pleased that some of the members who answered questions received affirmation and compliments on their answers. He thought that such interaction can be a positive factor in building the kind of board he had pictured.

Mark was not impressed with the practice of a board member being listed as a reference for prospective employees. He wondered why a person would choose a board member as a reference if the applicant were expecting to be evaluated on credentials.

As he reflected on the total session, he concluded that asking experienced board members to respond to new members' questions could be a valuable team building experience but he thought it should be done under the guidance of a proven facilitator like Larry who could correct misconceptions. He decided that it could be disastrous to do otherwise since many board members that he knew would promote and praise very harmful practices. He was thankful that this session had been positive and helpful rather than harmful.

Questions for Discussion

1. How do you regard the practice of prospective employees listing a member of the board as a reference?
2. What potential pitfalls can you identify in using experienced members of the board to instruct new members of the same board?
3. What value do you see in inviting experienced board members to share as follows: I once thought..., but now I think...? Or, I wish I had known then what I know now about...?
4. What information about a fellow member might help you and others in becoming a better board? How might certain information hinder growth?
5. How might sharing stories of decisions which were not so good be useful?

CHAPTER 11

Working With The
Board Attorney

NO ONE WAS surprised that Susan had the first question. "I have noticed when I attended board meetings before I was elected that the board attorney was always present. Is that required by law or what is the purpose of his being in attendance at all board meetings?"

"May I respond to that Mr. President?" Don asked. "That practice did not occur until I became president of the board. I felt that it was imperative that we consistently adhere to the law. No one on the board was an expert in the law so I thought that we needed our board attorney present at every meeting to warn us whenever, in the opinion of our attorney, we had started walking on shaky legal grounds. Also, I thought that it was important that we be able to get an instant legal opinion about issues that came before the board. I'm quite proud that for the last two years we've had legal counsel at every one of our meetings."

"I understand that you are quite proud that the school board attorney has been present at each school board meeting," Susan replied. "Now, I'd like to know the purpose of his attending the meetings. I assume that the board is billed for every hour he spends sitting here listening to us as we deliberate about all kinds of issues. I've been wondering, are we spending public funds wisely? Frankly, I'm surprised that Jerry hasn't been barking."

"We are involved in a lot of litigation," Don said."I like having him here to keep us from getting involved in even more litigation."

Ron, who had served on the board during the time Don was president, added, "I supported Don's motion to have legal counsel at each meeting. However, since one of the purposes of having him present at our meetings is to help us avoid litigation, I'm wondering why we've seen an increase rather than a decline in litigation? I'm not saying that we should blame Bob for the amount of litigation the board is involved with, but I really don't think we would've been involved in more litigation if he hadn't been at our meetings?"

"You raise a good point, Ron. I share Susan's concern, "Mark added. "Not only do I think it's not a wise use of our resources, but perhaps even more importantly, the board seems to rely on our attorney to tell us whether we should do something or not. I don't see that as a proper role of the school board attorney. When the Board wants to take an appropriate action, though there is an awareness that legal concerns are likely to be raised, it should ask its attorney to guide the Board to avoid legal missteps and reduce the prospect of litigation. The question: "Can the Board be sued" has an easy answer and it's 'Yes'. The attorney has the responsibility of aiding the Board to avoid legal entanglements while doing its work. What should the Board do is not a legal question. How should it do what it does may well have legal implications."

Don raised the issue of whether Lindell would be placed at a disadvantage if the board did not regularly have legal counsel at meetings. Lindell responded, "There are very few situations when we face a legal issue at a board meeting without any idea that it will be an issue. We have an agenda for each meeting and a policy provision that requires multiple readings to change policy absent an emergency. I discuss legal issues with our board attorney when I need his advice. I also have other legal resources available to me in addition to our board attorney."

"I am not trained in the law," Michael noted. "I do, however, have great respect for law and its role in the operation of our society. It seems to me that when we look to the law to tell us what we ought to do, we are looking in the wrong place. The law can help to clarify what we must do and what we may not do; it can never tell us what we should do. Our vision, related policy, and our best judgment provide answers to that question.

"As I think about it," Sylvia said, "I have another concern. I'm sitting here thinking about asking our attorney for a legal opinion while we're in a school board meeting. It seems tremendously unfair to him for us to do that. I'm leery of instant legal opinions and it appears to me that an instant legal opinion is far less likely to be based on solid legal grounds than the opinion we would get if we allowed our attorney to research the issue before he gave us an opinion. If we ask for an opinion in an open school board meeting, we put tremendous pressure on our attorney to provide an immediate answer. If he doesn't, the public might question why we have him as an attorney. I, for one, would prefer to have the attorney present only when we specifically ask for him to be present."

Michael admitted that the comments of the new board members made sense to him. He said that he thought that a knowledgeable school board attorney is indispensable but that the board attorney's most valuable work is outside a board meeting, not at the meeting. He said that he could see how it might be a win-win situation for the attorney and the board to have him present only when specifically requested and thereby allow adequate time for legal research before legal opinions are rendered.

Jerry jokingly warned that after hearing the discussion he might be barking at the next board meeting if the board continues to spend funds to have the school board attorney present unnecessarily. He went further to say that he had never even considered the wisdom or lack thereof in having the school board attorney present for every meeting of the board.

Michael cautioned Jerry that the school board attorney has been present because the board voted to have him there. He said that a vote of the board would be necessary to change the procedure. He suggested that it would be appropriate if one of the members might request to put the item on the agenda for the next meeting. He further noted that a current contract with the attorney must be considered in terms of any proposed changes in the relationship.

"I'm requesting it now," Jerry said to Michael. "Will you see that it's on the next agenda?"

"I can do that," Michael promised. "You may want to discuss it with Lindell and get some facts about the issue to support your motion. That will make it much easier for us to make an informed decision."

"Will do," Jerry responded.

"Please make it clear as you present your motion that there is nothing personal in this proposal," Susan requested. "I know that our board has confidence in Bob but I think the point that Sylvia made is very important. It's unfair to him for the board to ask for a legal opinion with no time to research the issue. I also concur with Michael's comment that a board attorney's most valuable work is outside a board meeting, not at the meeting."

Mark's reflection

Mark was encouraged that board members are showing a willingness to look at the ways we are doing things now with the possibility
of finding a better way to do them. He thought that it helped greatly
that Susan was calm and non-accusatory and that her suggestion was
clearly intended to make the board better, not to advance a personal
cause or discredit another member. He also felt that Jerry's humor
helped to keep the mood comfortable. Michael's point that the law
is not the source to answer the question of what we should do was
a strong factor and seemed to be well received by other members.
When the board chooses a course of action based on educational
wisdom rather than personal bias, legal counsel can effectively advise
as to ways that the action can be within the law.

Questions for Discussion

1. How might paying an attorney to be present at every meeting
   imply a responsibility to contribute an opinion on each item of
   business?
2. What advantages and/or disadvantages can you identify in having the board attorney present at all board meetings?
3. Can you think of a time a board wanted to do the right thing but
   did not do it because of the board attorney's advice?
4. To what extent do you believe that when the board chooses the
   right thing to do the board attorney should show them a legally
   correct way to do it?
5. Can you think of a situation when the threat or fear of possible
   legal action deterred a board from taking action that was otherwise warranted?
6. Mark said, "The board attorney's most valuable work is outside
   a board meeting, not at the meeting." Why do you agree or disagree with him?

CHAPTER 12

Rules Of Order For Meetings

"ONE OF THE things that bothers me most about beginning to serve on the school board," said Jerry, "is that I know very little about Robert's Rules of Order. I know that our board operates by Robert's Rules of Order, but frankly, it's too complicated for me. How can I learn what I must know about Robert's Rules of Order to be able to function as a board member?

"You are correct. We do operate by Robert's Rules of Order," Don said with pride. "When I was president of the board," he continued, "we adhered to those rules strictly. In fact, we kept our parliamentarian busy trying to see to it that we did not deviate from those rules of order. The public expects us to demonstrate that our board meetings are conducted in an excellent manner and I believe that includes following Robert's Rules of Order very closely."

"That's been a problem for our board, Sylvia observed. Robert's Rules of Order was designed to assist the efficiency of board meetings. We have allowed it to hinder our meetings. We do not need to haggle over rules and take the time and attention of the board. We have been far too nitpicky in this regard."

"Does the board use Robert's Rules of Order or does it use Robert's Rules of Order for Small Boards?" Mark asked.

"We just use Robert's Rules of Order," Don said."Are you suggesting that the size of the board makes a difference?"

"There is a major difference," Mark said. "Robert's Rules of Order for Small Boards (RROSB) is much less formal. Rather than being designed to use in conventions where formality is essential, RROSB is specifically designed to accommodate small boards like school boards.

"How does it make a difference?" Don asked."Could you give us some examples of the difference?"

"It allows the presiding officer to remain seated rather than stand. It allows the presiding officer to make or second a motion. It allows discussion before a motion is required and actually even permits the board to vote without having a motion or a second if the board chooses to do so. These modifications are intended to facilitate the meeting rather than hinder it as the regular Robert's Rules would do in meetings of small boards. I hope our board will choose to use the small board version of Robert's Rules."

"I hope so too," Michael said."It would sure make my life easier and I believe that all members of the board would feel more comfortable and be able to concentrate more on content than procedure."

"Would that require a policy change?" Susan asked.

"It most certainly would," Don said. "Our current policy specifies that the board will use the procedures specified in Robert's Rules of Order in all meetings, not Robert's Rules of Order for Small Boards. I am not in favor of changing how we operate. I've invested a lot of time in learning one set of rules. I don't want to start over now."

"I don't think it would cause you any problem," Mark said. "And it would be much better for the rest of us."

"May we propose policy changes at any meeting?" asked Susan.

"A policy change may be introduced at any meeting except at a special called meeting," Don volunteered. "However, because policy is such an important part of what we do, it requires two readings before it can be adopted by the board at the third meeting."

"Hold on a minute," Ron said. "I'm not a fan of Robert's Rules of Order but I don't want to do anything that would keep us from having motions in our school board meetings. We have always made motions and seconded them and that's the way our actions are recorded. I like a lot about the small board rules but I don't like that."

"I'm glad you raised that point, Mark said. "I don't like that either. I think putting things in the form of a motion helps to clarify what we are about to vote on. Fortunately, we can easily make that an exception to our operating procedure. In other words, we can simply specify that we will use RROSB except that we'll require motions and seconds. If there are other things about it that we don't like, we can exempt them also."

"Let's ask Lindell if he has any recommendation for the Board on this matter," Don said. "He seemed to be very satisfied with our use of the more formal Robert's Rules.

"You are all aware," stated Lindell, "that Robert introduced the Rules of Order to facilitate the conduct of business in organizations and associations. In a small board situation, such as meetings of a seven member board, it's much easier to keep up with what's going on to the extent that some relaxation of formality won't interfere with conduct of business. I'm certainly comfortable with the way you choose to conduct business - be it the formal rules or informal ones for small boards. Given the length of some of our meetings, allowing the president to remain seated would seem a plus, he joked."

"I hope we take action to change as soon as possible," Susan said. "I agree with Michael that such a change will permit us all to relax a bit more and concentrate on what we're trying to achieve rather than technicalities in the procedure."

Mark's Reflection.

Since he made the suggestion for Robert's Rules for Small Boards, he was pleased that it was well received. He has to be aware that his role in meetings is closely watched and most effective when it is moderate in scope and frequency. By asking others how they see the situation and asking their opinion, the quality of interaction improves.

Questions for Discussion

1. **Can you think of a situation where Robert's Rules of Order was allowed to hinder a board meeting?**
2. **What advantages, if any, do you see for your board using Robert's Rules of Order for Small Boards?**
3. **Are there members of your board who are intimidated by Roberts Rules of Order? If so, what can the board do to eliminate the problem?**
4. **Why might your board have a policy on meeting procedures that identifies the rules of order that will be used by the board?**
5. **Susan said that using Robert's Rules of Order for Small Boards "will permit us all to relax a bit more and concentrate on what we're trying to achieve rather than technicalities in the proce-dure." What is your assessment of that statement?**

CHAPTER 13

The Board Agenda

Getting an item on the agenda

JERRY RAISED THE issue of getting an item on the agenda." When I was campaigning," he said, "I made a list of things people brought to my attention that they thought the school board should do. I want to share that list with the school board, although it might be best to do it one item at a time. My question is, how do I get an item on the agenda?"

"Our board has delegated the duty to develop the agenda to the executive committee made up of the board president and the superintendent. Any board member can request to add an item to the agenda," Don said. "We have a board policy that requires that such requests be received by either the board president or the superintendent seven days in advance of the meeting. The policy also specifies that the superintendent and the board president – as the executive committee of the board – decide whether or not to put the item on the agenda. If they decide not to put the item on the agenda, which seldom occurs, you may request that the item be added at the beginning of the meeting. To add an item that the executive committee did not add requires a majority of the membership of the board."

"Why would the executive committee decide not to put an item on the agenda when it was requested by a member of the board?" Jerry asked, " Are we subject to censorship by the executive committee?"

"Sometimes, there are legitimate reasons not to put an item on the agenda," Sylvia said. "It's really not censorship. The board president and the superintendent sometimes have information that we don't have. Seldom do they fail to include items on the agenda that are requested by school board members but they frequently do not add items to the agenda that are requested by a private citizen."

"Does a majority of the membership mean a majority of the total board members regardless of how many members are in attendance?"Jerry asked.

"That is exactly what it means," Michael answered, "In the case of our board, it means four members."

"That provision prevents a minority of the board from adding an item to the agenda and acting on it in the unusual case that only four members are in attendance. Then, three members could take an action that they know a majority of the board opposes." Sylvia added.

"I fully understand that the board has lots of issues to discuss and lots of matters which require action," Susan said, "I don't want to put an item on the agenda and have the board pass over it quickly without giving it adequate consideration. Some matters that I will ask the board to consider are not urgent. They are important, but not urgent. What happens to my issues when the important gets pushed aside by the urgent?"

Annual Agenda

"That wouldn't be nearly so likely to occur if the board used an annual agenda," Mark responded. "That's what Larry suggested that we do during our retreat. He said that items could be added at any time and scheduled for discussion when the board meeting agenda was expected to be lighter. I think it would be a great help in ensuring that the board considers what it wants and needs to consider rather than letting things of importance to us get pushed aside."

"I've never heard of a school board that uses an annual agenda," Ron asserted. "And frankly, I don't see any advantage in using one. I have never had any trouble in getting anything that I've requested on the agenda for a school board meeting."

"The primary purpose of an annual agenda is to ensure that we don't get so busy with issues that arise that we fail to focus on things that we either want or need to consider," Mark explained. "For example, suppose that a board member suggests at a September meeting that we revisit our policy on coaches who are not full time employees of the school district. The board wants to do that but not now when we have so many other things going on. We can agree to add the issue to the annual agenda and determine the most appropriate time to consider the issue. When that time comes, it will automatically be added to the agenda and the administrative staff as well as others who need to be involved in the discussion will be prepared so that we can make an informed decision. If we don't have an annual agenda, we could forget to consider the issue and whoever requested that it be reconsidered would feel that their request was ignored or "put on the back burner."

"So are you saying that an annual agenda is basically a tool for helping the board organize its work by spreading the discussion of issues over the year so that we can adequately consider them in a timely manner." Jerry asked.

"That's exactly right," Mark responded.

"Since the example Mark gave had to do with policy, it occurred to me that it might be a good idea for us to schedule a review of a small section of our policies periodically on our annual agenda," Susan suggested. "If we reviewed the entire policy manual every four years, it would keep them current and every member of the board would have the opportunity to have input into every policy."

"Now look!" Ron objected. I've already told you that policymaking is my least favorite part of being on the school board. Now, you're suggesting that we do it at every meeting. I don't want to discuss every policy we have. I want to do less policy making, not more."

Consent Agenda

Sylvia, in an effort to unruffle Ron's feathers, explained, "Ron, we can do what Susan is suggesting without reviewing policy at each meeting and even at those meetings when we review a section of the policy manual, we can simply add "Review of Section such and such" to our consent agenda. If no one has a proposed change to a policy in that section, the policy review can be accomplished without discussion."

"That sounds much better to me," Ron replied. "I could live with that."

"What if a board member has a proposed change?" Susan asked.

Michael responded, "Then, when I call for a motion to adopt the consent agenda, you simply request that 'Policy Review' be removed from the consent agenda and we'll move it from the consent agenda to some place on the agenda where the proposal can be considered by the board."

"Why does it have to be moved," Jerry asked. "Why can't we discuss it where it is?"

"Because items on the consent agenda are either approved without discussion or moved from the consent agenda," Michael responded. "Things are put on the consent because they require board action but no discussion because all board members agree. That's why it's called the consent agenda-all members agree or consent to approval. Using a consent agenda saves time for the board. They are all approved with one motion, no discussion and one vote."

"I'm for anything that saves time and cuts the length of school board meetings," said Ron. "We should have been doing this a long time ago."

Mark's Reflection

Mark was pleased with the discussion. He concluded that if new procedures were presented patiently and understandably to the board, they had a chance of being adopted by the board. He determined that he would contain his frustration with members who seemed set in their ways. He also decided that explaining things understandably and using examples was worth the effort. After all one of his and other board members' major responsibilities is presenting ideas to other members and to the general public in such a way that could not only see the merits of the idea but support it.

Questions for Discussion

1. **What are the advantages of using an annual agenda?**
2. **What are the advantages of using a consent agenda?**
3. **Do you see ways that a consent agenda might be misused?**
4. **What should be the requirements for getting an item on the agenda?**
5. **How should a citizen be able to get on the board agenda?**

Chapter **14**

Building A School Budget

MARK REQUESTED THAT one of the members of the board take a few minutes to describe how the school board is involved in developing the annual budget for the school district. Michael asked Don if he'd like to handle that request. Don indicated that he'd be happy to summarize the process. He suggested that other members add comments and ask any questions they have following his summary.

Don explained that the school board sits down each year with the superintendent and administrative staff and goes over the current budget item by item. The board considers where it has under budgeted and over budgeted. Then, the superintendent informs the board about all recurring expenses which the board is obligated to pay. The superintendent explains changes in funding available from federal, state and local governments. He observed that the board spends hour after hour in these sessions going over the budget with a "fine-toothed comb." When funds are inadequate to fund the continuation of current programs, the board faces the necessity of making a decision as to what programs or services to cut. If there are discretionary funds, the board decides what programs or services to add.

"How does the board's vision impact the budget?" Mark asked.

"To be honest, we've not directly associated the two since I've been on the board." Don admitted. "Are you suggesting that they should be related?"

"If they aren't," Mark replied, "It seems that the vision is not a compelling one. I'd like to have the school budget built around our vision for the school system. I think that if our vision is a compelling one, the community will get behind it and take responsibility to provide the necessary funds."

"The way we've done our budget has worked for the fourteen years that I've been on the school board and it worked long before I became a member of the board," Ron said. "Let's don't start fixing things that aren't broken."

"We should always be looking for a better way to do things, Ron," Sylvia said. "We'll never get to be a better board by doing things the way they've always been done. I know you want both our board and our schools to be better don't you?"

"I've always been in favor of improvement in our schools, Ron said," but I'm very slow to support change."

"I'm in favor of having our budget reflect our vision but let's be certain that we build a budget that is fiscally conservative," Jerry requested. "Vision tends to get a little fluffy. I can support asking for funds for things that are absolutely necessary but I want to be certain that there are no pork barrel projects included."

Don bristled noticeably at Jerry's comment and sharply responded, "You won't find any pork barrel projects in the budgets when I was board president. And, "he continued, "In fact, I can assure you that there has not been a single pork barrel project in any budget since I have been on the board."

"I am more familiar with the bond issue passed two years ago," Jerry said. "It seemed to me that there was a little bit of sugar in the bond for every area of the district. I know there was a weight room at the high school and a covered outdoor play area at an elementary school and other special projects at other schools."

"Are you suggesting that the weight room and the covered play area were pork barrel projects," Don asked sarcastically.

"I don't see either one of them as essential to the education of our students. So, yes I am," Jerry responded.

Michael interrupted the strand of discussion by suggesting that the board's time would better be spent by looking forward at things we can do rather than spend time looking back at things we can do nothing about.

Susan agreed but she cautioned, "There are things we need to learn from past budgeting mistakes." She suggested that capital expenditures such as the ones that Jerry pointed out should be part of the regular 'pay as you go' budget instead of part of some bond issue our children will be paying on as adults." She challenged, "Let's have the courage and honesty to be transparent with the public by proposing what is needed to fulfill our vision in our budget rather than hiding things in a bond issue."

Jerry agreed. He said, "We may have to bond for a new school soon, but if we reject pork barrel projects when we pass a bond, we could pay off our debt, quit rotating bonds and our children would have a completely fiscally sound school district when they become adults." He added, "Imagine how our district's example would serve as an example to other districts and state leaders."

Sylvia supported the idea. She said, "We should reject the notion of putting our children in debt for things we can pay for today. If we need bonds to accommodate growth, so be it. But let's give future generations the benefit of having learned from our mistakes. Let's pay as we go for everything we possibly can."

Mark added, "We have signed on to be champions for children. That means that we'll articulate our vision and speak out strongly for what is needed to provide them with quality education." He continued, "It's a challenge to get the funds we need to provide a quality education for every child in our school district. We need unanimous board support for our budget. Then, we have to go into our communities and convince our friends and neighbors that our budget represents a worthwhile investment in education. We believe it and we sell it. That's community leadership. Remember, we don't react to public opinion, we create it. And the public opinion that we create now is that this budget will result in quality education for our children."

Michael wanted the conversation to end on a high note and he felt the conversation had gone as far as it could without further information from the staff. Attempting to close the conversation, he said "It seems clear that the majority of the board wants there to be a direct relationship between our vision and our budget and that we have a responsibility, once we adopt our budget, to wholeheartedly support it in the community."

Then Michael asked, "Lindell, could you and your staff give some attention to this issue and make some specific suggestions about how the board and staff might best work together in building public support for our school budget?"

"We can do that," Lindell replied. "It may be a good thing that I'm retiring. This board keeps finding new things for me to do," he continued jokingly.

Mark's Reflection

As Mark reflected on the conversation about the school budget, he was struck by how long-serving members of the board are sometimes defensive of the way things have previously been done. He thought that he would use a strategy of giving credit for what had been done and presenting new ideas in a way that built upon what had been done rather than suggesting that the previous way should be discarded and replaced by something new.

He was pleased that steps had been taken to move the board toward the notion that support for the budget should be unanimous so board members could lead the community in a single direction and create the opinion that the budget would result in quality schools. He concluded that such conversations were best if they preceded rather than followed adoption of the budget.

Questions for Discussion

1. **What are some ways the board can build support for the school budget?**
2. **What should be the relationship of the board's vision and the budget?**
3. **How might a board achieve budget equity in capital projects? Should that be the responsibility of the Superintendent?**
4. **What is your reaction to Ron's statement, "The way we've done our budget has worked for the fourteen years... Let's don't start fixing things that aren't broken."**
5. **What merit do you find in Mark's reflection: "He thought that he would use a strategy of giving credit for what had been done and presenting new ideas in a way that built upon what had been done rather than suggesting that the previous way should be discarded and replaced by something new?"**

CHAPTER 15

The School Board As A Learning Community

"WHEN WE TALKED at our retreat about vision and a picture of what we want to become," Susan shared, "I began to wonder about a picture or metaphor this Board might use to think of ourselves. It would be interesting and, hopefully helpful, to consider a term that would come to mind when we think of ourselves."

Perhaps a bit bothered by some of the topics Susan raised, Ron responded, "I've thought about that too and I would like to suggest the term "school board" to help us picture ourselves.

"You are almost too much sometimes, Ron," Sylvia responded, "I have not thought much about it, yet I can see some value in such an exercise. Susan, what metaphors come to your mind when you think of our board?"

"The usual ones- team, organization, corporate body, collective, and alliance- come to mind and none of them really speak to me," Susan responded.

"Agreed," Sylvia replied. "They lack something. When I was still teaching, our school generated a lot of school culture when we decided to operate as a "Professional Learning Community. Can you see any energy around the metaphor of our Board as a Learning Community?"

"Learning Community?" replied Jerry, "That does not ring my bell. Voters in my district elected me because of what I know-not for what they hoped I was going to learn while on the Board."

"You aren't telling us that you don't intend to learn anything more, are you, Jerry?" quipped Michael with as much lightness as he could muster for the occasion.

"Not at all," laughed Jerry. "Sometimes I operate as a learning machine. I just don't want to tell the public that I'm still learning. I think the community might lose some of the respect it has for me."

"I like the metaphor! " responded Susan with noticeable enthusiasm. "I can't believe how much I've learned since becoming a member of this board. And, I'm excited about continuing to learn throughout my time on the board."

"Before I agree to characterize our Board as a 'learning community,' I would like to know a lot more about what that means," cautioned Don. "New ways of thinking and talking are not threatening to me. Those of you who know me well will not be surprised to learn that I am not fond of 'buying a pig in a poke'."

"I think that I should make an intelligent statement on this topic," Jerry added. "Unfortunately, I don't have one ready yet. Perhaps, if Mark or Lindell or one of you other members would explain what a learning community is or what it would mean to this Board, I could respond more intelligently."

Lindell, who usually listens but seldom responds to Board conversations, responded to Jerry's invitation, "As Sylvia reminded us, several of our schools are considering the Professional Learning Community (PLC) as a way to enhance our focus on learning and student success. Having seen dozens of reforms come and go, I am a bit leery of 'magic bullets' and thought that this might be another in a long list. As I joined some of our professional development activities, I soon realized that PLCs are different and actually call for a change in the way we see ourselves and our mission."

Lindell continued, "The power in PLCs comes from the fact that it is not something else we do; it is rather a different view of who we are. The 3 big ideas of PLCs, according to recognized authorities and authors DuFour and Eaker are: Focus on Learning; Building a Collaborative Culture; and Results Orientation. I strongly commend the efforts of schools (and maybe, school systems) to operate as PLCs. I know much less about school boards becoming learning communities. The idea could hold some intrigue."

"Our Board would not try to be a PLC, since we are a lay board," Mark noted. "It would require a shift of perspective for a board to view itself as a community (with all that term implies) of learners. I suppose that many of our colleagues view boards as being in the business of encouraging others to learn, with little attention to our own learning. It is a fascinating topic to talk about. One of my favorite writers is John Gardner, whose thoughts and writings helped to prepare schools to think of themselves as PLCs (though he did not use that term), wrote long ago:' The most important contribution the school can make is to be a community in its own right.' Community is not a new concept and has much potential as a metaphor for schools, this board, and our district as a whole."

Mark's reflection.

Though he did contribute more to the discussion than he had intended, he was generally pleased with the meeting. He is intentional about his desire to contribute without being dominant by talking too much. The conversation is lively and several members have used humor to avoid offending another and even to smooth over some edgy moments. The tone of the interaction suggests that the board is becoming something of a community with more work to be done. He recalled with a smile the time in an earlier superintendency when he began a new school year by announcing to the staff and the larger community that it was his intention to learn more than anyone else during the next year - to be the principal learner. Some of his best staff members were a bit reluctant at first to think of themselves as learners- after all they had "terminal" degrees.

Questions for Discussion
1. **How realistic is it to talk and think about a school board that sees learning as an intentional activity of the board and its members?**
2. **When a board endorses learning as something of value for adults of the system is it likely to actually promote the practice?**
3. **How do the words we use and the metaphors we choose to think of ourselves make a difference in who we are and how we operate?**
4. **How can an individual board member help the board to view itself as a learning community?**
5. **Discuss the implications of Mark's comment: "I suppose that many of our colleagues view boards as being in the business of encouraging others to learn, with little attention to our own learning."**

CHAPTER 16

Accountability In Public Education

MANY THOUGHTS RACED through the mind of Mark Trent when he received an invitation to speak at a Chamber of Commerce summit on Accountability in Public Education in Progress County. One of the first images crossing his fertile mind was that of the Biblical story of Daniel in the lion's den.

He dismissed the thoughts conjured up by that image, not because they were inappropriate but, because they were not helpful in accomplishing the purpose for which he was willing to undertake such a challenge. He knew, even before the Chamber representative clarified the agenda, that he would be in a position of defending both the accountability stance of the system and the test scores from recent applications of the state standardized testing model. The mention of Progress County in the title for the summit was a clear indication that he was not to address the generalities of public education-but, the specifics of education in OUR county.

Perhaps, it was his basic faith in the willingness of the public to examine all sides of an issue before "locking down" a position to defend against all comers that motivated Mark to take on an "opportunity" such as the one now presented to him. Certainly, he remembered many occasions in which this basic faith was not supported by evidence.

Maybe, his ability to believe against evidence was a powerful force in keeping his enthusiasm at a high level. For whatever reason or lack of reason, he chose to renew his basic faith in the public's willingness to examine issues with both open minds and commitment to the common good. He had learned, sometimes through painful experiences, that people do not rise to lowered expectations. He chose to frame his outlook as "treat people 'as if' and not 'as is.' "

Realizing that he was engaging in one of his favorite activities of reflection and reframing, he chose to leave that enjoyable pursuit to "get on" with the task before him and to prepare for his role at the summit. One of the preparation techniques Mark has used with some success, and thus an attractive option for this activity, involved identifying some of the positions and/or premises likely to be held by those at the meeting. The following positions and expectancies were identified as likely:

- promoting charters and vouchers
- advancing Common Core State Standards(CCSS)
- questioning recent standardized test scores of local students
- comparing our students with Singapore and Finland, and maybe, Shanghai
- getting rid of bad teachers
- differentiated pay for teachers based on student test scores
- innovation and technology...replacing teachers with technology
- students as "human capital" or "assets"
- reform as deregulation and privatization
- public schools and teachers not willing to be accountable
- raising test scores to improve our economy

The compilation of this list tempted Mark to refer his invitation to someone on the payroll, rather than a Board member. The Pogo admonition that "there are no problems- only opportunities" was enough to create the impression that he was faced with an "insurmountable opportunity." An even casual review of the list revealed a strong perspective that those at the summit would hold views dramatically different from his own. This reflection was sufficient to show him that reframing would be in his best interest and in that of The Chamber.

Recognizing that these people are not enemies of education; rather they are among the leaders of our community who are there to support efforts to improve and expand our success in all endeavors. He remembered how they and the businesses they represent had financially supported everything from yearbook ads to bond issues. With much improved outlook he continued his preparation. He realized that he could not do everything needed to promote the good of public education, but he could do something'

He reminded himself that his purpose is less toward getting Chamber members to change their minds and/or their positions and more about openly and honestly representing public education as the best chance we have to shape the future of our society in the direction that we want to go. He reasoned that an improved awareness of the complexity of our society and our educational system will prepare one to adopt a more enlightened position on complex issues. The work of German social researchers (Rittel and Webber) who, in 1973, coined the term "wicked problem" came to his recollection.

A Short History Lesson

Perhaps, we could better understand today's "wicked problem" of education if we took a short recall of some of our history, Mark reflected. Back in 1914, Congress, concerned with workforce issues, funded programs to support vocational and industrial education. The great depression and the 1930s saw a New Deal with the Civilian Conservation Corps(CCC) and other programs to offer jobs and job training to young adults.The 40s saw life adjustment education and the 50s featured a back -to-basics focus on teaching the skills needed to learn - the well-known 3Rs.

In the 1960s we were told that the schools were "too academic" and we moved to more freedom and spontaneity. The 1970s brought a sharp increase in minimum competency testing and another "back-to-basics" focus. In the 1980s, "Nation at Risk' (1983) was published and, though seriously flawed, motivated decision makers to call for increased graduation requirements and other standards, more testing and more comparing results, and a big-time focus on accountability.

Since 2000 the debate continues with advocates of whole-child education being set versus more high-stakes testing in rather narrow areas and more talk of accountability. The major disconnect between these views seems to be widening. TED.com facilitator Adam Burk opened a lively discussion on a simple question about the "purpose of education."

After 365 respondents identified 365 rather different answers the invitation to respond was closed. Common Core State Standards seems to be a rather bold move to bypass the conversation and "force" on American education through economic and political strategies, a set of standards developed by a very few without the benefit of public discourse. It remains to be seen whether the standards will benefit education since there has been little to no field testing. In more recent times the Common Core train has "jumped the track" a few times as some of the applications of the inadequately researched project have been tried on our students with resulting questions raised for newer attention.

A continuing challenge for public education is the inclusion of all, or nearly all, of our people- at a time when many seem to be "giving up" on educating all of our youth and concentrating on those of most interest by securing their presence in the "lifeboats." Charter schools and vouchers are a favorite approach by those with such views and values. Feeling less confident than before these thoughts, he again chose to reframe. This shift led him to the question raised by the late Ron Edmonds: "How many successes for those difficult to educate are necessary to show that they can be educated?"

Mark decided to look forward to the opportunities offered by the summit and to openly and honestly focus on two operational principles of his past administration: 1) We will be transparent in our operation so those who choose to make some effort will be able to understand what is going on and 2) Those involved in the operation of the system will accept and practice accountability for resources used and results achieved

At the Summit

Approximately 250 people showed up at the summit. An air of anticipation and expectancy was obvious to those who chose to recognize it. Public awareness of the meeting and its announced purpose resulted from promotion among the media in the community. The participants were seated at round tables with 4-6 persons at each. A microphone and lectern were provided for principal speakers and a 'roving mic' was provided to facilitate comments from persons at the tables. Mark had discussed the arrangements with the Chamber representative well in advance.

Presentation by Mark

"Your gracious invitation to join you for this significant Education Summit is greatly appreciated. To be able to focus on public education while interacting with our citizens allows me to combine two of my favorite activities. It is my intention to share a few remarks about my personal approach to this opportunity and then to engage with you in lively Q&A.

As I prepared for this anticipated opportunity for us to positively influence the future of public education in this county, I employed a mental model which has served me for many years. This model asks me to **Reflect** on my experience with education in this community and elsewhere. Having been a student, teacher, coach, principal, and superintendent, parent and now board member does not qualify me as an expert- but it does make me quite experienced. As an aside those of us who value reflection should become more competent each year as we have another year of experience to work with. The 2nd step of the model is to **Focus** on the task at hand- which was done for me and shared by the Chamber: "Accountability in Public Education in Progress County." The 3rd step of the model is to **Connect** with key individuals and organizations- this is now in process.

The story of public education is really many stories told in many voices by many people. Each of these stories -some told and some untold- is a valid one. Perhaps, one of the factors preventing us from realizing the full potential of these stories is our inherent tendency to value some of these stories more than others. One of the things we can do today is to look at our collective story through the lens of accountability, as the Chamber has asked us to do. If accountability requires transparency, let us also view through that lens.

With responsible and transparent participation of all present today we can accomplish much of the agenda of the Chamber. Please do not attach the name/s of individuals to complaints or criticisms. In an attempt to hear from more people, I ask you to take the time allotted to present to your table group topics or questions of interest to you and do initial processing there. Choose in succession those topics to share with the larger group. In the next 5 minutes, please do a bit of organizing and process comments to select your first item to share. Other instructions will follow."

Mark's Reflection

Mark was neither surprised nor disappointed in the direction taken by participants at the summit. The usual items that come up in such a setting, came up. He was pleased that he was able to use his facilitating skills to focus on those topics that could be influenced by the persons present. Those topics resulting from actions by authorities at another level, were identified with reference to how to influence action there.

Some of the topics indicated things that Mark saw as progress; recent reversals in approval of Common Core gave hope for wider participation and field testing in setting standards; an increased awareness of the importance of education to the business community (widely represented at the summit); more willingness to listen to the stories of others.

Some of the topics Mark saw as areas of needed attention; residual command-control directives in education; lifeboat thinking to promote vouchers, charter schools and elitist programs; calls for more testing of more people; favor for using influence to force others to go our way; too much us-them thinking; few awards and honors for students like ours; heavily- funded organizations to oppose democratic practices in schools; inadequate funding for programs proven to have a good chance to work with the more challenged students in our schools.

Of all the things speaking to him as challenges, Mark chose three on which he could personally work:

1. To do everything he could to enlarge the winners circle, thereby allowing more and more students to succeed and to reap

the benefits of quality education (the implications of quality education not to be overlooked.

2. To Intentionally promote and circulate more stories that expand the old ones where "people like us can't do things like that" (he remembered the stories from his youth that saw "two kinds of students-those who were good at school and those who were not." If there are no stories in which persons from your group have succeeded in school or life, what chance do you have? At least, we have made gains in gender equality. Though we have more work to do. Some of our students have been 'storied' to see themselves and their world as 'apart'; he wants to help find or create stories that think it back to 'whole.'

3. To promote the awareness that increasing diversity in organizations, including school systems, is a strength rather than a problem. He remembered having gone as a younger superintendent to conferences with sessions on such topics as: "Dealing with the Problem of Increasing Diversity." He thought how sad and self-defeating was such thinking and framing.

Questions for Discussion

1. What are some ways to work effectively with individuals and organizations known to differ in goals and methods from those of the school system?
2. When individual school board members are invited to speak to clubs or other groups, what should they consider in their decision on whether or not to accept?
3. What responsibility, if any, does a board member have to represent and speak for the board when speaking to a group of citizens?
4. How did Mark build support for Progress County Schools through this activity?
5. What value do you find in the FOCUS-REFLECT- CONNECT Model that Mark presented at the Summit?

CHAPTER 17

Should We Ban The Book?

WHEN SCHOOL BOARDS take on the issues related to the possibility of restricting or even banning books and other reading materials available to students, the level of public interest skyrockets. This is a truth that is going to garner the attention of our Board in the "twinkling of an eye."

Progress County Schools and their Board were having a relatively calm and productive year when a small bombshell exploded around the issue of a proposal to remove a book from the approved reading list for high school students. Some parents became disturbed when they received a warning that the approved reading list for their teenagers included Catcher in the Rye-a book known to include questionable language and behaviors not generally recommended for high school students. Many in the community had already taken sides when the issue appeared on the agenda of the Board at the request of Jerry.

Carefully prepared materials were distributed to show that the book was a classic tale of teenage angst which could help students to adjust to the challenges of that difficult time in their lives. Just as convincing was a well-prepared counter that suggested that other books dealt with the topic in ways that did not use profanity and sexual references. Further, the counter argument noted that it is possible for a person to be well educated without reading Catcher. Good citizens of intelligence and character were available to speak to each side of the ban or don't ban issue. "Is this the issue that will reflect the measure of the Board's community leadership?" wondered Michael as he prepared to address the topic on the Board agenda.

To begin the discussion at the board meeting, Michael introduced Mary Hopkins, chairman of the English Department at Progress County High School. He reported that he had asked her to give a very short overview of the book to introduce the discussion of the topic at the school board meeting.

She said, "The Catcher in the Rye tells the story of Holden Caulfield, a rebellious teenager facing psychological trouble. He was expelled from his school when he was 16. He took a trip to New York City. On his journey, he experienced alcoholism, constant cigarette smoking and emotional breakdowns. He rejects middle class values and pretty much does whatever he thinks of. Holden talks in 50's slang and constantly uses vulgar language.

A Pastor's Comments. J. Barker Thompson, pastor of Faith Is the Victory Church, had signed up to address the board on the issue. He was the first speaker. He pointed out that he had more than 100 supporters with him. In dramatic fashion, he used his five minutes allowed by board policy to proclaim that the decision facing the board was a "no brainer." He almost shouted, "This book is a primer for vulgarity and contains cuss word after cuss word! If you want to teach our children profanity, it's the perfect textbook!"

He said that the profanity includes all kinds of swearing with multiple use of the F-word. "There are few sentences in the book that do not have a cuss word. It deserves to be banned for its profanity alone. It uses the Lord's name in vain 200 times and the young man about whom the story is written does blasphemous acts from the front to the back of the book. That is a second reason to ban the book."

Holding up three fingers, he declared that a third reason to ban the book is that "the main character makes statements against minorities, women, and the disabled. He even makes immoral statements about phonies."

Lifting four fingers, he said, "A fourth reason to ban the book is because it has multiple scenes and references to prostitution, premarital sex and alcohol abuse."

He concluded by asking, "Who among us wants to see our young people behave like this young man? Can't we find books with worthy models for our precious, but sometimes gullible, teenagers?"

A High School Senior's Comments. Alicia Barker, a high school senior, spoke next. "Catcher in the Rye is my favorite book. It captures the essence of being a troubled kid, which most of us have experienced at some point. Catcher masterfully captures the mentality of depression and the process of dissociation from society. It is a portrayal of the psychology of a 16 year old who has recently been disillusioned by the security of adults and adulthood, which used to give him a sense of security. His most compelling wish is to save kids from growing up. That's where it gets its title. Holden has a fantasy about kids in a field of rye beside a cliff running around and he is the catcher. He must catch them if they are about to fall off-into the clutches of maturity. Anyone who is judging the book by the main character's merits is missing the point to the story. It is a great literary piece and more people should read it and it certainly should not be banned by the school board."

Comments from a librarian. Erin Householder, a librarian at Progress County High School distributed copies of her remarks to the board and then proceeded to read them.

"Catcher in the Rye illustrates the alienation and separation of youth from adult society that began with industrialization and mass education and has accelerated with each generation until today, where adolescent young people live in a world completely apart from adult influence, taking their cues about morality and right conduct not from legitimate adult authority figures but from each other.

Catcher in the Rye provides many moral lessons that a student can learn from and these are based on education, religion, intolerance, and respect. For example, Holden is presented as being intolerant to everybody, disrespectful, and hateful and he hates the use of certain words. Yet, the lack of religion also makes him intolerant because he considers himself an atheist as he cannot cope with any religion. Besides religion, his intolerance is based on the fact that he has a problem with everyone since he lacks respect and does not admit to any mistake. Consequently, his intolerant personality is unacceptable in the society, and the book teaches that this is an undesirable trait.

Holden, the central character, has so much anger and hatred towards the world and there is no better way of expressing his anger than by using powerful 'bad' words. Take those words out and Holden would become a totally different person, possibly even too boring to keep reading. Salinger did an amazing job using words that are less offensive than others, and words that are part of many people's everyday language. Therefore, banning Catcher because of its use of offensive language is impractical; it's not like we are teaching words to children that they haven't already heard before.

It deals with issues such as profanity, irrational behavior, and teenage sex and has very vital and appropriate lessons to teenagers and youth as it teaches the benefits of tolerance, discipline, religion, and rational behavior. It in particular teaches the youth that desirable behavior is more beneficial to them than to society and as such, it should not be banned from high school curricula."

Board Discussion. Following public comments, Michael opened the floor for discussion by the board. Jerry began the discussion by saying, "As a parent I am greatly troubled by all of the bad language and sexual references throughout the book and many parents have told me of their concern and encouraged me to vote to ban the book."

"I share Jerry's concern," said Sylvia, "and I must balance it with an undying conviction that Freedom of Speech is a fundamental American right that must be preserved. I'm also struggling to find the proper perspective of how this issue relates to the long-cherished notion of academic freedom in educational settings."

Susan added, "The maturity and increasing responsibility of our students is another factor to consider. These are young adults, not little children." She continued, "When I talked with my niece, a high school senior, she pointed out to me that she and her fellow students could read Catcher and easily discern between dead-end behaviors and lifestyles and those providing models for us. 'Who wants to be like Holden? Give us some credit' was her comment. I think we should."

"Catcher is a filthy book in my mind," said Don. "My wife, who is a teacher strongly disagrees. She says that it is such an important book in American literature, that banning it is just keeping students away from one of the best books ever written. I don't see it that way, but she's a good teacher and out of respect for her, I can't vote to ban it. As much as I hate to abstain on any issue, I'm going to have to do it on this one."

Michael observed, "The idea of banning a book is dreadful to my mind. At the same time, I don't want to force students to read a book when their parents have a legitimate reason to object to it. I want to protect the right of parents to opt out for their children."

Michael directed his next comment to Lindell, "What guidance or professional recommendation can you give this board as we deal with this matter."

Lindell told the Board about the review hearings at the school and the involvement of students, staff, and parents with a clear message in favor of academic freedom. He noted that the staff respected the authority of the Board to make a command decision on this matter and yet, prefers that the Board leave the matter of selecting reading lists to the processes currently in place.

Lindell continued, "You have shown awareness of the important values to be protected in this matter and the balancing necessary. I believe that the interests of the school system will best be served by denying the request to remove the book from the reading list," Lindell responded.

James Williams, Regional Director of PTA was present. Michael invited him to share the PTA position on the issue. Mr. Williams reported that the PTA had a long-standing position favoring academic freedom. However, he suggested that parents should be able to opt their children out of required assignments to which they had legitimate objections.

Lindell reported that current administrative procedures allows parents such an opt out procedure. He added, "If it pleases the board, our staff will draft a board policy to establish a procedure for parents to request approved substitutions for required reading materials and certain other educational matters they find objectionable." He said the policy would be ready for the board's consideration at its next meeting.

After more discussion and sharing, Susan made a motion to decline the removal of the book while affirming support for parental right to choose. The motion carried with a 5-1-1 vote.

Michael reminded the board that it had determined that it would from time to time briefly reflect on controversial decisions the board had made. He suggested that this decision was exactly the kind of decision that called for an all-important time for reflection and sharing of lessons learned. He asked for a volunteer to kick off the time of reflection.

"This is not the first time I have been the only member voting as I did," shared Jerry. "I listened to the position expressed by each person who spoke but I was not persuaded to change my mind on this issue. I would vote the same way again on the issue. However, the first time that I felt that the other members of the Board listened to my position and accepted the fact that I am voting my conscience without making me feel that I'm not a good board member."

Susan noted, "When battle lines are drawn on an issue, there is a tendency to look for evidence supporting the position already taken. It requires some effort to listen for wisdom in the opposing argument. I thought all board members listened."

Mark added, "We saw tonight that being an effective board requires a balancing of values and rights rather than just weighing them to find the preponderance of evidence."

"The issue left me in a bind," noted Don. I responded by remaining neutral and abstaining. I honestly don't feel good about how I handled it. I think that each of us as board members need to find a way to come to a decision and vote on every issue we face. I will try to do that in the future except where there is a conflict of interest."

"For me," Sylvia observed, "it was a matter of finding a way to protect something we value- decency and parental rights, while respecting other values-academic freedom and faith in our young people to make intelligent choices. That's what Mark calls 'balancing' I guess."

"As a board, we took the matter before us seriously and made a decision that we can explain and stand behind, "Michael stated. "I trust that we will do the same each time we face such an issue."

"I had friends and neighbors who urged me to vote on each side of the issue," Ron said. "I think that after our discussion today, I won't have to avoid either side. I can explain our action to each group. I like being in that position."

Mark's Reflection

On his way home from the meeting, Mark thought that it was becoming more clear that the Board, after being uptight about public reflection, was gaining proficiency with the process and, further, it began to appear that the public was responding more favorably to a Board with the courage to do at least some of its collective reflection in the public eye. There seemed to be a new kind of openness and freedom around publicly identifying things we are learning. He was anxious to learn if members of the public whose position was not supported by the Board would, in fact, be influenced by the shared thinking of members as they deliberated toward a decision. He was not completely sure exploring multiple points of view around a complicated issue would please the whole community. As a parent he recalled discussions with Maggie about their responsibility to balance "preparing their children for the world in which they would live " with "protecting them from that world."

Questions for Discussion

1. **What do you think of the board's decision?**
2. **How did the board's discussion help the community to understand the decision?**
3. **Neither Don nor Jerry voted with the majority. How well do you think will be able to explain and support the decision of the board?**

4. What do you think the community reaction to the board's decision will be?
5. How important is it to clarify the issues of "protecting our kids" vs. "preparing our kids" in a discussion such as the one before the board?
6. How do openness and transparency in the decision process contribute to the response of those opposed to the decision?

CHAPTER 18

Termination Of An Employee

SUPERINTENDENT SHARP SENT a memo to the board advising the members that Della Snyder, a former special education transportation assistant had appealed her dismissal to the Board of Education. Mrs. Snyder had been a special education transportation assistant for eight years. Her record was good. Although it contained no special commendations, neither did it contain negative comments about her performance.

On February 8, 2019 after the bus had made its last stop to pick up children in the morning the bus broke down. Another special-education bus was sent to pick up those children to take them to school. In the process of transferring all the children on the bus, Della was apparently distracted and did not perform her duties to check to be sure that all the children were secured safely. One 9-year-old girl who was both physically and mentally challenged did not have her wheelchair secured. As the bus moved toward the school, her wheelchair overturned and her head barely missed the corner of a divider on the bus. The girl was not seriously injured but her parents, as well as several other parents of children who rode the bus, were upset considerably by the incident.

As a result of the incident, Della was fired. She has now employed an attorney who has made an argument in his request for an appeal that this was the first negative incident in Della's tenure with the school system. She was remorseful and had pledged that such an incident would never happen again. She appealed her termination to the board and was requesting reinstatement. The issue was the next item on the agenda of the regular meeting of the board. Michael called on her attorney, Proctor Upchurch for the presentation of her appeal.

Mr. Upchurch introduced himself as the attorney for Della Snyder in the matter of her termination by the school district. He summarized the facts of the case essentially in agreement with a memorandum sent out by the superintendent. Then, he asked the board to overturn her dismissal and reinstate her to the position she had held for eight years.

"Della Snyder has been a trustworthy and faithful employee of the Board of Education for eight years. She has performed her duties without fail during this rather long period of time. She knows the children who ride this bus because she has worked with this driver and with this bus during her entire time of employment with the school district. She knows the students and they have confidence in her. She loves the students. She is extremely distressed about the accident and has a renewed commitment to be diligent with regard to student safety. She needs this job and the board will be well served by keeping her working as a transportation aid for special education. She is available to return to work immediately and the board will not have to train someone else to fill the position."

Michael asked for comments or questions from members of the board. Ron spoke first, "Mr. Upchurch, did Mrs. Snyder understand that being certain that all children were properly secured in their places was a part of her responsibility?"

"Yes sir. She did," Mr. Upchurch replied.

"Do you believe that neglecting to fasten the child's wheelchair properly is a serious breach of duty?" Ron asked.

"Mrs. Snyder understands that it was her duty and that she should have done it and she is seriously remorseful that she did not fulfill that responsibility," He replied.

"Were our school administrators justified in terminating her employment?" Ron asked.

"We are not arguing that Mrs. Snyder did not commit a breach of duty. We are here to assure the board that she has learned a tremendous lesson from the experience and that she will be a better employee because of it. She has contacted the child's family to apologize and express her deep regret. We're asking for a second chance for Mrs. Snyder and we're promising that, if given a second chance, this board will not regret its decision."

"Failure to properly secure the wheelchair of a disabled student on a school bus is a serious breach of conduct in my opinion," Susan said. "I think our school administrators were justified in terminating her for that breach. However, I see merit in Mr. Upchurch's argument that Mrs. Snyder might be a better employee now than she has ever been. And, it appears that she has been a good employee for a long time. I would not oppose giving her a second chance. We don't have to train her and she is available immediately to get back to work."

Don weighed in with the comment that, "If this board overturns the decision of our school administrators, I'm afraid that it will have a negative effect on their morale. I've always thought the board should support its employees."

"Mrs. Snyder was a long-term employee," Sylvia said, "What about the board's support for her? I've been given a second chance a few times and in each case I dedicated myself to prove I was worthy of it. I believe that Mrs. Snyder will do the same."

Michael turned to the superintendent and asked, " If the board were to overturn the decision of administrators, how would it affect them?"

Lindell smiled and said, "Our administrators think that their action was justified and I agree that it was. They would be concerned if the board ruled that the action was not justified. I haven't heard any board member or even Mrs. Snyder's attorney argue that the action was not justified. If the board deems that the action was justified but decided to give Mrs. Snyder a second chance, I'm confident that our administrators will neither be disappointed nor feel that the board has failed to support them."

"I agree that the failure to secure a disabled child on the school bus is breach which probably justifies termination under the law," Mark said, "but the law sets a floor below which we cannot go. It is not the standard that this board should use in making decisions. We do not want to send a message to our employees that the first time you mess up in the school system you'll automatically be fired. I know that our administrators join the board in appreciating our employees and what they do for our children every day. I concur with superintendent Sharp that they would not be upset by giving Mrs. Snyder a second chance."

"Mr. President," Mark continued,"I move that we reinstate Mrs. Snyder to her job as a special education transportation aide effective immediately with the provision that the superintendent have a letter of reprimand placed in her personnel file to remind her of the seriousness of this offense."

"I second the motion," Don said. "I want our board to support all of its employees, not just its administrators as I implied in my initial remarks."

After the motion was carried unanimously, Michael reminded the board that at the retreat they had agreed to reflect upon important decisions and list what they had learned from them. He asked the board to take a few minutes for reflection and to share learnings.

Don began by suggesting, "I hope the entire board has learned one of the things that I have learned that it's important for the board to support all of its employees not just its administrators."

Ron observed that, "The board doesn't have to fire someone just because it's justified or even because the law allows it. The board should do the right thing, not the easiest. I believe we did the right thing in this case."

Susan added that, "When it is possible to salvage a good employee, it is a win-win situation for the board and the employee."

Michael said he was pleased to observe that, "An effective board can often find the path with a heart."

Mark observed, when our board approaches an issue with an open mind, members feel empowered to change their minds and we are much more likely to reach a decision that the entire board can support."

Jerry said he learned that," We shouldn't just do what the law allows us to do. We should live above the law and do what's right."

Sylvia closed the comments by saying, "One of the most valuable things I learned was the value of our board reflecting on the decisions we make. Every comment made by a member of our board will help our community to understand and support our decision. This was a powerful activity and, I believe that this exercise has helped us to grow as a board."

Mark's Reflection.

He was well pleased with both the action of the Board and the public reflection on what was learned from the experience. The honesty and openness of all parties contributed to a favorable resolution. Asking the Superintendent for the response of administrators was important. The question arises: Should our policies and practices provide for an employee to appeal actions without the necessity of employing counsel? Was our conversation about learning communities helpful in publicly recognizing the value of learning by staff. Mark was pleased with an emerging sense that learning by everyone-not students only-is the business of the district.

Questions for Discussion

1. How did the comments made by board members in their time of reflection help the community to understand the decision of the board?
2. If you were a member of the Progress County Board, would you have voted to reinstate the transportation aide? Why?
3. When such a decision is made, how important is it to validate those making the original decision while choosing another consideration for board action?
4. If competing values that lead to different actions are considered, why is it important to focus on the values rather than the individuals?
5. How do you think the community will react to the board's decision to offer Della Snyder a second chance?
6. In what ways did the unanimous agreement that the behavior in question was unacceptable make it easier to offer a second chance?

CHAPTER 19

Selecting A Superintendent

IT DIDN'T MAKE much difference where Mark went in town, he was frequently bombarded with questions about how the board intended to select a new superintendent. Harman Threet apparently was lying in wait for him when he came into the Red Rooster for breakfast. "I've been waiting for you to show up this morning. I have some advice for you," Harman said with what seemed to be a sense of urgency. "I hope the board won't waste money on conducting a search for a new superintendent. We have exactly the person our school system needs right here ready and raring to go. I don't see how we could hope to have a better superintendent than Harry Canfield." He paused as if he were waiting for Mark to thank him for the brilliant suggestion.

"I believe that our board is committed to finding the very best person we can find for the job," Mark replied. "We're excited about the opportunity our board has to select a leader for our school system. We aren't taking that responsibility lightly. I'm not going into this selection process with a preconceived notion about who we will select. I'll promise you this. I'll vote for the person that I think will do the best job leading our school system to provide the educational opportunities that our children deserve."

"Good! That means I can count on you to vote for Harry," Harman said with a laugh as if he were joking but Mark knew he wasn't. He continued, "You won't find anyone better."

"Maybe not," Mark replied, also with a laugh but he certainly didn't think it was funny.

Waitress Margie Barnes, who overheard the entire conversation, advised Mark that it didn't matter as much to her who was selected as long as the board chose a local person. "We don't need a superintendent who doesn't understand this community and its people," she said with enough confidence that any listener who overheard the conversation would have no doubt that the matter was now settled. "Surely we don't need to go outside this county to find a person qualified to lead our school system, she reiterated."

"She's exactly right," Marvin Sysco chimed in from the next table. "Johnson County hired a superintendent from Michigan and now they're trying to figure out how to get rid of him. I think they'll end up buying out his contract. When you choose a local candidate you know what you're getting."

Mark hadn't really come in seeking advice on the superintendent search. He enjoyed coming to the Red Rooster for breakfast once or twice a week. He liked chatting with the locals about what was going on around town, especially in the schools, but it appeared on this issue he was going to get more advice than he really wanted.

The school board had discussed this issue thoroughly. There was considerable disagreement among the membership of the board about whether to do a search and if so whether the board should do it or hire a consultant. They had come to an agreement that they would hire a consultant and had interviewed three, including one from the State School Boards Association. They opted to go with the School Boards Association because the price was reasonable and, after all, the board was a member of the association and it existed to help its members. It would be there to help the board through any difficulty it may have with the superintendent it selected. That was not necessarily true of the other search firms. Clark Perry, the Executive Director of the School Boards Association, had agreed to lead the search. He was well known and popular with the board.

It was not a unanimous vote. Ron had felt strongly that the board did not need the assistance of a search firm. He thought it was a total waste of taxpayer dollars. He had his own candidate and it certainly wasn't Harry Canfield. Ron's son, Jimmy, had been suspended twice by Harry and constantly seemed to stay in trouble at school. Harry Canfield would've been Ron's last choice to be superintendent of schools. He would have voted for an outsider first.

Both Jerry and Susan were concerned that the school boards association seemed to recommend the same candidates in multiple districts. Susan said that she had heard that the association showed favoritism toward certain candidates and seemed to be committed to finding them a job as a superintendent. The majority of the board felt that the school boards association had a vested interest in the board finding an outstanding superintendent and they liked the fact that the board had a better chance of holding their own association accountable for the results of the search. It didn't bother them that candidates were sometimes recommended in more than one district. It seemed reasonable that a good candidate in one school district might well be a good candidate in a similar school district.

Four of the board members, including Mark, had attended a clinic at the School Boards Association's annual meeting on superintendent selection. They learned how complicated the process of superintendent selection could be if done correctly. Advertising, receiving applications, answering questions for candidates, checking references, running background checks and contacting people who were not given as references but who were in a position to know the candidate's strengths and weaknesses, handling all the correspondence, conducting preliminary phone interviews and many other details of a superintendent search were too much for school board members to do.

Information had also been shared in the seminar that an individual or organization conducting a search on behalf of the board had much more freedom under the "sunshine law" than did the board or its members. Another advantage that a search firm has is the ability to recruit candidates without their invitation to apply being misinterpreted as commitment to support the candidate recruited, as might be the case if a school board member recruited a candidate.

They also had been warned that the credibility of information gained from references and other persons who know the candidates well is affected by the credibility of the person conducting the inquiry. People who are knowledgeable about a candidate's performance are frequently reluctant to share negative information with people they don't know they can trust to keep their identity confidential. Negative information, if accurate, could be a showstopper. Much better to learn such information to prevent a person from being hired rather than after the person is hired.

The board asked the Association to engage the community in the selection process by conducting several meetings to hear from participants about expectations for the position. Based upon results of the meetings, the Association would recommend a set of criteria for the board's consideration and adoption. The Association also agreed to advertise the position, recruit quality applicants, receive applications, process them and recommend the five best candidates in terms of how well each met the criteria established by the board. The association agreed to provide a summary of the qualifications of each candidate recommended and even provide a set of sample interview questions based specifically upon the criteria adopted by the board.

In preparation for the interviews, each member of the board was assigned a criterion and had responsibility to ask questions related to that criterion in the interview. The questions related to the criterion were to be selected from those recommended by the association or developed by the board member who would be asking the questions related to the criterion. Each board member was provided a scoring sheet to complete during the interview. The purpose of the scoring sheet was to help individual board members organize their reactions to and rank each candidate's responses during the interview. Each score sheet was marked: "For Your Eyes Only."

The board agreed that each member would keep a score sheet for personal use in ranking candidates. After the completion of interviews, each board member would list the candidates in rank order. The rankings were to be averaged to select the "tentatively preferred" candidate. The consultant, on behalf of the board, would begin contract discussions with the "tentatively preferred" candidate. There would be no announcement that the candidate was the "preferred candidate." If the preferred candidate were agreeable to the terms offered by the board, the consultant would share information with the board attorney who would draft a contract for consideration by the candidate. If the contract is agreeable to the candidate, the board will approve the contract and elect the candidate. If agreement cannot be reached the same process will be repeated for the next candidate.

Larry Houston had suggested this process when Mark had called to ask his advice on the superintendent selection process. Larry observed that boards frequently feel like their search is over when they identify a top candidate. "It isn't over until it's over," Larry warned. "I've seen many boards blow the process after they have identified their top candidate. The board should not consider a candidate the top candidate until the board offers the job and it's important that the board only offer the job to one candidate."

Larry said that the process he recommended would allow the board to determine whether or not a candidate would accept the job before the board officially made an offer. He reminded Mark that far too many candidates apply for jobs in order to increase their salary and strengthen their contract in their current position. He recommended the process because it serves the board well but does not allow candidates to misuse the search process. When Mark explained Larry's recommendation, the board adopted the process unanimously.

After the board meeting where the candidates were accepted unanimously, Mark was rather excited to share with Maggie the results of the school board meeting. "I can't believe that our school board has handled this process so well," he shared with her. "The board adopted the process that Larry recommended. It unanimously accepted the five candidates recommended by our consultant even though none of the candidates were local and the members agreed to each ask questions related to a specific criterion in the interview. I'm asking myself: was that really our board?"

"What was the issue with local candidates?" Maggie inquired. Did you expect that to be the source of some controversy?"

"I know that some of the members of the board strongly preferred a local candidate," Mark responded. "I would like to have some local candidates myself," he continued. "We have two employees who could do the job well but neither of them want it. So, we honestly don't have a local candidate who wants the job who has the experience and skills necessary to move the school system forward."

"Two of the board members had a specific local candidate that they seemed committed to, although neither supported the other's candidate," Mark observed. "I'm shocked that they didn't raise the issue."

"That seems like a really good thing to me," Maggie said. "Maybe they recognized the importance of the board's responsibility to select the best superintendent and they're willing to let go of their personal preferences for the good of the school system."

"I hope so," said Mark."I hope so," he repeated. "If that's the case, our board is moving in the right direction much faster than I ever expected it to move. But, when the board behaves like this, it's actually fun to be a board member."

Things weren't quite so rosy the next morning. Mark just finished eating breakfast when the phone rang. It was Michael Garcia. "Mark, sorry to bother you so early but I've been on the telephone for 15 minutes talking with Ron. He wants the board to reconsider its action to accept the five candidates recommended by Clark Perry. He wants to either ask him to put the best local candidate in the search or for the board to choose one itself."

"That's ridiculous." Mark said. "We can't do that! Have you talked with any of the other board members?"

"No, but Ron had already talked to Jerry before he called me," Michael said disappointingly. "He said that Jerry also regretted that the board had not insisted on having local candidates."

"Well, I certainly don't," Mark said, "and I hope no other board members are having second thoughts."

"We've already accepted the five candidates as finalists," Michael said. "We can't change that! However, I don't see any reason why Ron couldn't make a motion to add a local candidate to the five finalists. Do you?"

"I think a strong argument could be made that the board had excluded every other applicant when it accepted the five presented by

Clark Perry," Mark responded. "It's clearly too late to add any local candidates who didn't apply before the deadline, but I don't think we should use technicalities to keep the will of the board from being done. I suggest you let him make the motion and see what happens."

Michael agreed.

"I'm amazed at how some people's opinion can turn 180 degrees simply because someone disagreed with them," Mark observed. "It appears that Ron, who was a champion for children last night, lost his nerve when he met a little opposition."

"That's been one of the most disappointing things I've observed since I've been a member of the school board, Michael said. "It hurts to see a school board member who knows what's right, fail to stand up for it because someone disagreed with the action of the board."

"When does Ron want the board to consider the question of adding a local candidate?" Mark asked. "Is he requesting a special called meeting?"

"No. He wants to do it when we select the candidates for contract discussions," Michael said." If his motion carries, It will really complicate our process."

"I know Ron doesn't want Harry Canfield as a finalist. He'd be risking that if he makes that motion," Mark observed..

"He certainly would," Michael said."I hope he realizes that before he makes the motion."

Off and on for the next couple of days, Mark thought about the questions that he would ask the candidates for superintendent. He never expected to go through this process again as a member of the school board so he wanted to be certain that he used this opportunity to do it right. He'd been assigned the criterion, "Exercises strong and effective leadership for the school system." He determined that he would prepare four questions in priority order. Hopefully, he would get to ask all four questions but if not, he wanted to ask the most important one first.

He asked Maggie and several friends what they felt would be the single most important question he could ask to determine whether or not a candidate would be a strong and effective leader of the school system.

Tony Taylor, Mark's barber, suggested the question: "As the leader of our school system, would you be more like Mahatma Gandhi or Douglas MacArthur?" He had a pretty good explanation for his question but changed his mind before he completed his explanation to say that upon reconsideration, the question he would ask was, "What would your barber say about you as a leader?" He found his own question to be hilarious and it didn't take long for the entire barbershop to join him in hearty laughter. Mark was glad to be a party in bringing a higher level of mirth than usual to the barbershop.

Ray Griswold, the mayor, said he thought a good question would be, "What do you promise to accomplish in our school system in the first 100 days after you become our superintendent?" He suggested that any candidate who didn't say that he or she would primarily listen, should be eliminated. He concluded that a person who is unwilling to listen would never be an effective leader.

Jess Hawkins, a butcher at Kroger, suggested that the most important question regarding strong and effective leadership would be, "How will you determine which practices or services are wasteful and how will you decide whose position should be cut if that becomes necessary?" Mark asked Jess if he thought that his line of work inspired his question. Jess admitted that it might have had some impact but he considered the ability to cut budgets to be a basic function of leadership.

Maggie's one question was, "Tell us about a significant failure that you have experienced as a leader and what you learned from the experience?' "She said that it's important to have a leader who recognizes and admits failure and even more important to have a leader who learns from reflecting on experiences. Wisely, for a number of reasons, Mark didn't hesitate in promising Maggie that her question would be one that he would ask the candidates.

The meeting had already been set for Saturday morning when the board would select the first candidate for contract discussions. The plan was to select two candidates from five candidates for contract discussions. Fortunately, Ron had decided by this time that his motion to add a local candidate was not a good idea. However, he kept his promise and made the motion but it was disposed of without discussion, dying for lack of a second.

Interviews with the candidates went smoothly. Mark thought the board seemed fairly sophisticated in the way it handled the process. Michael kept the board on task and the process moving at a steady but unrushed pace. Remarkably, seldom did a board member attempt to use the occasion to philosophy or to "chase rabbits" but when they did, Michael quickly brought the focus back to the issue.

Michael asked each board member to name their top two candidates in no particular order. All board members had Carter Bragg's name among their top two candidates. "I think we have our man," Michael suggested.

"Hold on!" Ron objected. "He was not my first choice."

"Nor mine," said Don and Jerry almost simultaneously.

"I don't think that matters," Michael said. "That's the beauty of how we're doing this. He is either the first or second choice of every member of the board. No other candidate has anywhere close to as much support from the board."

Sylvia made a motion to ask Clark Perry to discuss the provisions of the contract the board had drafted with Carter Bragg. She carefully avoided identifying him as the board's top choice because the plan was to offer the position to only a candidate who had already tentatively agreed to the terms before the board voted to offer a contract. The board was determined not to have its superintendent be the second or third candidate to be offered the job.

The next day, Clark called Michael to tell him that he had explored the provisions of the contract with Carter Bragg and that they were very close. The salary offered was acceptable to him but he was concerned about two provisions in the contract. The first was a provision requiring that the superintendent live in the district. The board had proposed the following language:

The SUPERINTENDENT shall reside within the boundaries of the school district throughout the term of the contract. The contract will be voided if the SUPERINTENDENT does not meet the residency requirement.

Carter said that he would like for his wife and children to continue to live in their current home until they were able to sell it. He planned to return home each weekend until they sold the home and moved into the school district. Although Carter's plan was to stay in the district during the week his primary residence would not immediately be within the boundaries of the school district.

Michael informed Clark that the school board had thoroughly discussed a tentative contract and that the board was unwavering on the requirement that the superintendent live within the school district. He said that the board felt that the highest-paid person in the school system must certainly be a taxpayer in the district. He said that the board had agreed to allow up to three months for a candidate to move his or her family into the school district but living in the district full-time was not negotiable.

Carter's second concern was a provision for terminating the contract for cause. The board's draft contract contained the following language that had been suggested to the board by Larry:

This Employment Contract may be terminated by the BOARD for cause upon sufficient proof of improper conduct, inefficient service, neglect of duty, or failure to follow BOARD directives and policies. If the BOARD terminates this Contract for cause, the SUPERINTENDENT will be entitled to no further benefits or compensation.

Carter preferred the language that was in his current contract as superintendent that required the board to pay the full salary and benefits for the remainder of the term of the contract if the contract was terminated regardless of the cause.

Michael chuckled and told Clark, "I can see why he would prefer that language but the board is absolutely committed to doing everything in its power to keep from continuing to pay any employee, including the superintendent, who is terminated for cause." Michael continued, "Tell him we really want him to come be our superintendent but if he intends to be terminated for cause we would appreciate him staying where he is."

Late the following day, Clark called Michael to say, "I think that you have found a superintendent." He advised Michael to call a special meeting of the board for the purpose of approving the contract as soon as possible.

"What about the two provisions he objected to?" Michael asked.

"He said that he could live with the three-month provision to move his family and that your point was well taken about being terminated for cause," Clark said with a smile. "He said that being terminated for cause was the least of his worries and, in fact, after he thought about it he admitted that he would strongly oppose continuing to pay any other employee dismissed for cause. He said it would be hypocritical of him to have a provision in his contract that would require him to be paid if he were terminated for cause."

"I'm beginning to feel more confident that we selected the right candidate," Michael said." I know the board will be excited."

Mark's reflection

As he reviewed the events around the selection, he was reassured that clearly expressing the intent of the Board before naming and candidates or specifying locals was helpful. He understood the sentiment in favor of selecting a person from the community as one who knew the district, but continued to wonder why something such as experience in the district- something possessed by every employee- would be sought as if it were rare and valuable. The use of a consultant was of prime importance. Community meetings, background checks, and questions to be asked in the interviews all helped. Honesty and transparency throughout the selection process were factors that added credibility and confidence. The experience was evidence of how the Board had matured.

Questions for Discussion

1. When should the board conduct a search for a new superintendent?
2. What are the advantages and disadvantages of using a consultant to facilitate the search for a new superintendent?
3. How does a bit of levity, or even moderate humor, sometimes help when members see things very differently?
4. How were openness and honesty contributing factors in the board being able to arrive at a tough (for some) decision?
5. Discuss advantages and disadvantages of local candidates being in a position to lead effectively?

The Board's Relationship With Its Superintendent

Michael reminded the board he had previously been charged by the board to schedule a session to discuss the board's relationship with and expectations for a new superintendent. He said that Lindell had agreed to participate in the first part of the program to offer his perspective on the relationship. He requested that Lindell share the most important aspects between a school board and its superintendent whether or not it was part of the relationship that he had with this board.

Lindell began by saying the most important element of a board- superintendent relationship was mutual respect and trust. He said it takes awhile to develop but not long to destroy.

"Would you share with us how you believe that is developed," Sylvia asked.

"It requires that neither party spring public surprises on the other," Lindell continued. "It also requires honesty and openness and a commitment on the part of all concerned not to attempt to discredit or embarrass the other."

"The second element in the board-superintendent relationship is the combination of appreciation and encouragement. So many school boards today offer little or no encouragement and appreciation what-soever to their superintendent. The members of the board seem to always find something to criticize but never anything to praise. The performance of the superintendent and the relationship between the superintendent and board are both greatly enhanced by encourage-ment and appreciation."

"It's very interesting that you would choose that as the second most important aspect," Don said. "I think that you will acknowledge that I made a special effort during the two years I was Board President to publicly recognize and compliment you and the staff."

"There is a difference between compliments and encouragement. Compliments that are deserved are encouraging; superficial compli-ments aren't encouraging and they don't help to build trust. When a board member says, 'We're always delighted to hear a report from the best superintendent in the state, it seems a bit insincere and that is not very encouraging. On the other hand, when a board member says, 'We appreciate the careful planning and hard work done by our superintendent and staff to help us increase our reading scores, it seems sincere so it encourages us and we deeply appreciate it.' "

Michael thanked Lindell for sharing these observations. He expressed appreciation to board members for interacting about this matter. He said he thought it was a very important issue for the board to consider now before it begins to establish a relationship with a new superin-tendent. He asked Lindell if he had additional advice for the board.

"The board should genuinely want its superintendent to succeed and board members should do everything in their power to make the su-perintendent successful," Lindell said. "This doesn't mean that board members must agree with the superintendent or support all recommendations coming from the superintendent. Even board members who vote not to renew or even to terminate the superintendent's contract, should continue to support the superintendent as long as s/he holds that position. To do otherwise, is harmful to the school district, its employees and the students it serves.

Susan agreed. I think that makes perfect sense. I consider it to be unethical for a school board member to make derogatory remarks about the superintendent. That just tends to make him or her less effective. Our board, individually and collectively, should be committed to making our superintendent be as effective as possible so that our school district will be the best it can be for our children."

Ron didn't quite see it that way. "I can't support someone whose contract I already know what I'm going to vote to terminate. If we make a superintendent look good when we've already decided to terminate the contract, it's going to make the board look bad. Frankly, if someone's going to look bad, I'd rather it be the superintendent than the board. We have to run for reelection. The superintendent doesn't."

Don made an attempt to help Ron understand. "I think the point is even if a superintendent's performance merits termination of his contract, the board should continue to do what it can to make this school system operate effectively and efficiently. That includes helping the superintendent to be effective until relieved of responsibilities."

"I understand what you're saying," Ron replied. "I just don't agree."

"It seems to me that most school boards and most school board members either do not understand or do not agree," Lindell said. "It may be a hard lesson for school board members, but the bottom line is this: A school board cannot be effective unless it has an effective superintendent."

Susan was surprised if not shocked by Lindell's statement. " That's a strong statement," Lindell. "I'm going to think about that some more. But, I'd like to know if you think it works the other way."

"A superintendent can be effective even if the board is not effective," Lindell replied. "But, a superintendent can never achieve maximum effectiveness without a good school board."

Mark was still struggling to be certain that he did not speak more than his fair share. He certainly did not want to dominate the discussion. He had strong opinions about this subject as he did about most subjects related to the school board. He judged it was time for him to contribute to this discussion. "Our board needs to commit to supporting our superintendent consistently. It is unethical for a school board member to make derogatory remarks about any employee of the school system throughout the entire time the person is employed by the school system. Criticism of employees by board members diminishes the employee's effectiveness as well as the school system's ability to serve its students. This is especially true of board criticism of its superintendent."

Ron could hardly sit still as Mark was finishing his comments but he didn't interrupt. "I can't believe you're saying that we don't have a right to criticize the superintendent. The superintendent is the only employee who reports to the board and we need to tell him or her when we're dissatisfied with what's going on."

"I didn't say board members shouldn't tell the superintendent about the dissatisfaction with what's going on," Mark said. "There is a big difference in talking to the superintendent about expectations and telling citizens in the community about our dissatisfaction with the superintendent's performance. We should do the first but never the second."

Lindell agreed with Mark. "That's exactly right, Mark. it's not uncommon for school board members to criticize their superintendent in the community and then expect him or her to be effective in leading the school system. If your superintendent deserves to be fired, then do it. Please don't keep a superintendent in your employment and criticize him or her in the community. You are shooting yourselves in the foot– or more likely, in the head."

"That makes sense if you think about it," Sylvia agreed. "I don't think that school board members who do that ever think about the problem it causes. I'm very hopeful that our board will be careful not to do that."

Mark's Reflection

Mark thought that this session was well received by all board members and that it would result in a better relationship between the board and superintendent. He believed that every member sincerely wanted to make the board's relationship with its superintendent as strong and effective as possible. He thought that Lindell's statement that "A school board cannot be effective unless it has an effective superintendent" had grabbed the attention of every board member. He speculated that the statement was the subject of much reflection on the part of his fellow board members.

Questions for Discussion

1. **What do you think of Lindell's explanation of the difference between compliments and encouragement?**
2. **Where do you come down on the disagreement between Ron and Mark about criticizing the superintendent?**
3. **How might it be helpful for a board and superintendent to discuss a potential situation before it becomes a reality?**
4. **Books have been written on Board- Superintendent relations; what do you think are the essentials for success?**
5. **How much value do you assign to social opportunities for interaction of board members and superintendent when minutes are not taken?**

CHAPTER **21**

The Senior Prank

HIGH SCHOOL GRADUATION was rapidly approaching in Progress County. Considerable excitement was in the air. All in all, the Progress County Board of Education had done very well. Margie's articles that mentioned the Board of Education had for the most part been very positive. Board members had certainly disagreed on issues, though they had done so in a civil manner. Without question, public confidence in the board was on the increase.

Mark and Maggie were at home just finishing dinner with his nephew and his wife when the phone rang. Jack Scott apologized for calling Mark in the evening at home and said, "I think this is how it's supposed to work. When I have a major problem, I call my school board member. Is that right?"

"In an ideal world," Mark said, "you have a problem, you call your school principal. If that doesn't work, you call your superintendent. If that doesn't work, you appeal to the school board. You've already reached me now so, if you want to tell me your problem, I'll see if I can give you some guidance about how to handle it."

Jack was articulate and organized as he provided the following summary to Mark: "My son Darren is President of the Student Council at

Model City High School. He's a good student with a solid 3.8 grade point average. He has never been in trouble at the high school until now. He and seventeen other graduating seniors, including Ricky Jacobs, the senior class president, decided that they were obligated to carry on the senior prank. As you probably know, members of the senior class have pulled a prank at the school near the end of the year for as long as I can remember. We did it when I was a student there. The problem is, we have a new principal, Carmen Newsom, who has legitimately been trying to establish herself as a strong disciplinarian. She has told all eighteen of the students that, as partial punishment for their participation in the senior prank, they will not be allowed to participate in graduation ceremonies. Instead, they will be expected to come by the high school and pick up their diplomas the next day.

Both Darren and Ricky are scheduled to speak at the graduation. Nearly all of the students who've been excluded from commencement exercises have family members coming in to watch their graduation. Many of these family members already have purchased airline tickets. I don't object to Darren being punished but I think it's a tremendous injustice to deny him and the other students the opportunity to participate in graduation ceremonies. This is the culmination of twelve years of work for them.

We've already gone to the school to talk with the principal to no avail. We appealed immediately to the superintendent but he has informed us that he will not overturn the decision of the principal. We want to appeal to the school board but you don't have a regular meeting scheduled until after the graduation ceremonies. Can you help us get a special called meeting for consideration of this issue? It's tremendously important to us and we would deeply appreciate your assistance." Mark replied: "You won't need any assistance from me. We have a policy that makes the procedure available for any citizen of our community to request a special called meeting. The policy doesn't guarantee that you'll get a meeting but it establishes a procedure for requesting one."

"Did your group present either your request to the principal or your appeal to the superintendent in writing?" Mark asked.

"Our request to the principal was verbal as was her denial of our request. However, we presented a written appeal to the superintendent and he provided us with a written response," Jack replied.

"I suggest that you send a copy of your appeal and request for a special called meeting to Board President Michael Garcia with a copy to the superintendent and each member of the board. I would attach a copy of your appeal to the superintendent as well as a copy of his response. An emergency meeting requires three days notice so I'd send the request by email this evening. I'll support calling a special meeting if the matter comes to the board but the executive committee may choose to call one without polling the board. I understand your frustration and I'm very hopeful that we'll be able to bring this matter to a satisfactory conclusion for all."

Before Jack could respond, Mark asked," Did your group propose a punishment that you thought would be more appropriate than exclusion from graduation ceremonies?"

"We did not," Jack said.

"It may be wise to consider such a proposal in case you're asked," Mark suggested. "I'll let you go so you can get busy with your communications."

Michael was in favor of calling the special school board meeting to deal with the appeal to the board. Lindell was not enthusiastic about it but he didn't object so Michael asked him to send out a notice of a special called meeting.

The first special called meeting of the board as presently constituted was scheduled for 6PM on Thursday evening. All members of the board were in attendance and the meeting room was packed with students, parents and interested observers.

Michael began the meeting by thanking board members for making a special effort required to participate in a special called meeting for the purpose of considering an appeal from students and parents at Model City High School. He also thanked participants for coming and asked for each person in attendance who had never been to a school board meeting before to raise their hand. About three fourths of the group raised their hands.

Michael informed participants that this was a meeting of the board- not an open forum for public comment. He urged members of the audience to refrain from clapping, cheering, booing or showing approval or disapproval of comments made. He asked if the parents and students bringing the appeal had chosen someone to speak for them. They indicated that they had selected two people to speak – one a student and one a parent- so Michael invited the first person to speak.

Ricky Jacobs identified himself as President of the Senior Class at Model City High School. He delivered a well rehearsed speech with sincerity and emotion. His speech teacher should have been extremely proud. He said that a written account of the "Senior Pranks" at Model City High School over the last 26 years was contained in a document in the school library. He told how members of the senior class had felt an obligation to continue the tradition by performing such a prank.

He said that as president of the senior class, he had called a few leaders together to help plan and conduct a senior prank. He said that only a few students were invited because it needed to be done in secret and have the element of surprise. He told how each of the eighteen students had obtained two chickens and placed them in strategic locations throughout the school. Each student had previously prepared a humorous message to attach to a leg of each of the chickens that student had brought. He said that none of the messages contained profane or inappropriate language. It was all done in the spirit of fun. He said that the students had not anticipated an angry response from the principal. He said that they had apologized to her and had spent much of the afternoon and evening cleaning up the mess the chickens had made in order not to put such an unpleasant task upon the custodians. He closed his comments by saying, "We apologize for our actions and for causing you the inconvenience of having to take your time for the special meeting. We thank you for doing so and we beg you to allow us to participate in our graduation ceremonies. Our participation means a great deal to us and even more to our families and friends, many of whom have come from out of town to participate. We pledge to graciously accept whatever punishment this board deems appropriate but please do not deny us a reward that we have worked for at least twelve years to attain."

Michael told Ricky that the board appreciated his concise summary of the events. He even said that he was pleased to have the student appear before the board and be able to express himself in an articulate and thoughtful manner. Then, he asked if any member of the board had questions for Ricky.

Sylvia asked,"Ricky, as president of the senior class in a high school with a long-standing tradition of senior pranks – one in which the pranks are even catalogued in a document in the school library – would you organize a senior prank if you were faced with that decision again?"

"Honestly, I wish you hadn't asked me that question," Ricky admitted, "Yes! I must be truthful and admit that I would organize a senior prank again. I am, and I believe all of the students who participated in this prank are respectful of the authority of our school administrators. I think it's a harmless tradition so long as we don't damage any property or hurt anyone and, in this instance, we did neither."

"Then why did you apologize to the principal and now to the board?" Sylvia asked.

"I'm deeply sorry for the stress we caused for Mrs. Newsome, in her first year as our principal," Ricky said sincerely. "I'm also very sorry about the trouble and inconvenience that we have caused this board."

Jack Scott stood to address the board. He introduced himself as the father of Darren Scott, President of the Student Council at Model City High School. He emphasized that the students were carrying on a tradition at the school, that the students involved had carefully cleaned up the mess and that there was no damage to school property and no one was hurt.

"May I respectfully suggest that if Mr. Johnson who retired last year were still principal," Mr. Scott said, "this would not have been a significant incident. I do not say this to insult Mrs. Newsome. I respect her and fully understand that as a high school principal she wants to be certain that the students know that she is in control of the school. Otherwise, it would be easy for discipline to get out of hand. In this instance, her zeal to establish herself as a stern disciplinarian seems to have caused her to overreact and set a punishment which far exceeds the offense."

"On behalf of the students and parents involved in this incident," Mr. Scott continued, "I urge this board to overturn the action to bar the students from graduation exercises. Instead, set a punishment or allow her to set a punishment that is appropriate to the offense. That is the fair thing to do. That is the right thing to do. Regardless of the outcome, thank you for considering this matter."

Michael thanked Mr. Scott for his presentation to the board and asked if any board member had questions or comments.

"As I have listened to these presentations, I thought back to my high school days," Don said. "These students probably thought by looking at me that I was too old to be able to remember that far back," he joked. "I remember that, I participated in a high school prank myself. Our principal required us to wash every window – both inside and out – in our school because part of our prank was to write with white shoe polish what we thought was a clever message on one window in each classroom. Actually, the windows badly needed washing so, in effect, our school was better because we had pulled a senior prank."

"Having been a high school principal myself," Don continued, "my emotions are divided on this issue. I have been consistent, as a member of this board, in supporting our administration. On the other hand, I can't see how participating in this prank causes the students to deserve being denied the right to participate in their own graduation exercises."

"I feel an obligation to support Mrs. Newsome, especially when the superintendent has supported her decision," Jerry said. "Are we justified in not supporting our administrators?"

"For fourteen years, I've supported every decision of a principal regarding school discipline," Ron said. "We cannot afford to allow our students to think that they can do whatever they want in the school and suffer no consequences for their actions. I'm hopeful that this board will continue to consistently support the decisions of our school administrators."

"I think we should support our administrators," Mark said. "That doesn't mean we must always agree with them and uphold their decisions. Our board is committed to fairness in every situation. Fairness dictates that we do not come into a meeting such as this with a commitment to support the decision of an administrator. We want our administrators to make excellent decisions and when they don't, our best avenue of supporting them might be in pointing out why we can't support their decision. This provides guidance in making better ones in the future. If the board blindly supports bad decisions we can expect many more such decisions in the future. If we only support decisions when they are right, we'll get more wise decisions."

Susan thought it was time for the board to act. "I move that the Board instruct our superintendent to work with Mrs. Newsome to establish a reasonable and appropriate punishment for the students who participated in this incident provided that punishment does not include denying them the opportunity to fully participate in their graduation."

After the motion was carried, Michael suggested to the board that this seems to be another situation where the board could profit from spending five minutes in collective reflection upon what the board had learned from this experience. He invited members to share their thoughts.

Ron said that for the first time in his career as a school board member he voted against supporting a decision of a school administrator. He said that he'd learned that the board could support its administrators without necessarily agreeing with every decision they made. "I've supported some bad decisions in the past that I wish now I hadn't supported," he admitted. "I've gained some wisdom tonight," he concluded.

Jerry said that like Ron, he'd realized for the first time that the board could support its administrators without endorsing their every decision. "That, he said," is a lesson every school board member should learn."

Susan said that she was impressed with the way Michael conducted the meeting. She learned that laying out a few simple ground rules at the beginning paid off big time in the behavior of participants at a meeting.

Mark said, "I saw evidence that when a board, in spite of disagreement among the members, shows respect both for the opinion and for the person who held the opinion, the collective wisdom is able to guide the board to a good decision."

Michael observed that, "When the board operates in an atmosphere where board members are not threatened by expressing their opinions, members who otherwise might dig in and hold strongly to their opinions will sometimes change their minds. I commend Ron for maintaining an open-minded approach tonight and all members of the board for helping to create a non threatening atmosphere."

Since no other member offered a comment, Michael declared the meeting adjourned.

All eighteen students and their parents and friends who had come to support them remained seated quietly throughout the "collective reflection" activity. When the meeting was adjourned, each of the eighteen students as well as each of their parents and even some of their friends who were in attendance individually thanked the members of the board for hearing the appeal and for the decision they reached.

Mark's Reflection

Mark could not help but reflect on the meeting as he drove home. He thought that the board had taken a big step both toward becoming a more effective board and in improving the community's confidence in the school board. He thought that the few minutes the board spent in reflecting was an especially meaningful activity in not only help-ing the board to increase its effectiveness but also in giving persons in attendance additional opportunity for insight into the commitment of the board to be the best it can be. He thought the board was mov-ing quickly in that direction. Once again, he saw that the selection of a punishment, independent of admission of guilt, has an element of generational flavor. The respectful and sincere reaction of the students made it much more appealing to honor their request.

Questions for Discussion

1. To what extent do you agree with Mark's statement that fairness dictates that the board not come into a meeting with a commit-ment to support the decision of an administrator?
2. What did you like best about what happened at this board meeting?
3. How did the board contribute to or damage community support with this decision and the way the meeting was conducted?
4. How crucial was the honesty and openness of the students in admitting what they did and why?
5. How do you see Ron's admission that he gained some wisdom in terms of impact on other members?

CHAPTER 22

Religion And Schools

THE OCTOBER MEETING of the Progress County Board of Education was rocking along very well until it was time for the agenda item entitled "ACLU letter about religion in our schools."

Michael asked Lindell to introduce the issue and give some background.

Michael reported that the school district received a letter this week from the ACLU challenging what it called "ongoing practices by officials promoting and endorsing specific religious beliefs." It specifically mentioned the distribution of Bibles on school campus and during school time by the Gideons International, teachers leading religious songs and opening the school day with prayer, and teachers and other school officials posting Bible verses and other religious items in school classrooms and hallways.

Michael told the board that the letter also complained that a group called "Praying Parents" pray together in the school cafeteria as students arrive for the school day and then deliver personalized notes inside classrooms informing individual students and teachers that they have been prayed for.

"The letter concludes that individual parents and families- not public school officials- have the right to decide what sort of religious education their children receive," Michael said. "They have threatened to file a lawsuit if we do not stop these practices in our schools."

"Why would the ACLU or anybody else care that some of our teachers are leading religious songs and a prayer to help students start the day off right?" Ron inquired.

"If it were up to me personally," said Sylvia. "I'd have the students singing spirituals and reading the Bible at school. And also be trying to convert every one of them to Christianity because I'm an evangelical Christian. But I must admit that I would be one of the first and one of the loudest to scream about it if my grandchildren had a teacher of some other religion who tried to indoctrinate them or have them participate in activities promoting that religion."

"I would feel the same way, but this is America, a Christian nation," Don added. "We need to protect the rights of Christian teachers to freely express their religious beliefs. This country was founded for religious freedom. Our teachers have a constitutional right to freedom of religion. We need to fight this. Let the ACLU file a lawsuit if they choose. Constitutional principles are at stake here."

"You're right about constitutional principles being at stake," Sylvia added. "The Constitutional principles that are at stake in this case have been clearly set out in the Bill of Rights for over 200 years: Congress shall make no law respecting an establishment of religion, or prohibiting the free exercise thereof."

The leftist ACLU guys tend to forget about the "or prohibiting the free exercise" part an awful lot," Ron retorted. "I'm glad to see parents getting involved and showing an interest in children's lives. It's much better than them not caring. Why is it that students don't say the pledge of allegiance in school anymore? It's probably because the word 'God' is in it. The ACLU doesn't have a grip on the Constitution, they simply twist it into their own perverted version of what this country should look like. When did a democracy become what the minority wants rather than the majority? It wouldn't surprise me if they come up with some plan to sue the government to declare the winner of a political election to be the candidate with the fewest votes."

"The ACLU is really not the issue here," Michael stated, "it's about whether what we are doing or permitting to be done in our schools is the right thing to do. I strongly believe that decisions about religion should be left in the hands of families and faith communities, not public school officials. The constitutional principle of religious liberty is best protected when the government stays out of religion. I don't see how students can feel comfortable expressing their religious beliefs when they conflict with those that their teachers and administrators are imposing on them."

"You don't have to be a mental giant to recognize that freedom of religion ceases to exist when teachers, acting as agents of the government, use school time and a captive audience to engage in religious activities," Sylvia said.

"I hear what you're saying, but the superintendent just told us that the ACLU is objecting to parents coming to school to pray for teachers and the children who attend the school," Ron said. "We should be proud of that kind of support from parents. They are demonstrating their faith to their children. Please tell me what is wrong with that?"

"Ron, you know that there are many religious groups whose beliefs conflict seriously with those of Christians," Mark said. "Would you be willing to allow them to come into our schools and pray? For example, would you vote to allow Muslims to come into our school cafeteria and pray? Is it right for us as government officials to give certain individuals and faiths preferential use of school facilities? The ACLU's goal is to make sure that religious liberty continues to be a hallmark of our democracy. They do that by trying to make sure that the government stays out of deciding which religions to promote."

"Is a teacher posting a Bible verse like "Do unto others as you'd have them do unto you" in a classroom promoting a religion?" asked Ron. "It seems to me that it is just a reminder to students that they should be nice to each other. It's teaching morals, not religion. I honestly don't see anything religious about that Bible verse."

"I think that the ACLU would say that if it's in the Bible, posting it on a classroom wall promotes religion," Don said sarcastically.

"I hate the ACLU," Ron responded. "They persecute Christians and they are determined to get God out of government. America is a Christian nation and I'd sooner walk through hell with the can of gasoline than to see that change. Tell me one good thing the ACLU has ever done."

"I'm not an authority on the ACLU," Mark replied."but I know that the ACLU vigorously defends the rights of all Americans to practice their religion and express their faith, including public school students. I can mention a few cases that I know of in our neighboring states."

Mark continued, "For instance, in Tennessee they defended an elementary-school student's right to read his Bible at school during a free-reading period. In Virginia they supported the right of Christian students to proselytize on a community college campus. And, another time in Virginia, they supported students' right to wear t-shirts encouraging school-sponsored prayer. In North Carolina they fought to allow a 6-year-old to read a poem with the word 'God' in it at her school's Veterans Day assembly, after school officials told her that she had to remove the word."

"I never heard of any of that before. But, did you notice that they were going against the school board in every one of the cases that you mentioned?" Jerry inquired.

"Yes, I did, but the problem comes when school officials promote or show preference to a specific religion or deny students freedom of expression of their religious beliefs, Mark explained. "We need to understand, as Sylvia said earlier, that teachers, when they are acting as representatives of a public school system, are agents of the government. So during that time their individual rights are constrained by the Establishment Clause. When they are off duty, school employees are free to engage in worship, proselytizing or any other lawful faith based activity."

"So, Mark," Jerry inquired earnestly, "Do you believe that religion and God have no place in schools?"

"Absolutely not," Mark responded. "Students and staff need to bring their religion to school with them. I believe that schools are a laboratory for religion.They demonstrate their religion by how they treat others, how they conduct themselves, how they befriend the friendless, how they encourage those who are discouraged, how they share with the needy, how they defend the bullied, how they produce their best work and avoid misbehavior. They learn religious principles at home and in church, then, they demonstrate their religion and their relationship to God at school. There is no law against that." He continued, "Genuine religion is not demonstrated by carrying a Bible or wearing a t-shirt with a religious saying or cross around your neck, It is shown by the way we treat others."

"Thank you. Thank you," Sylvia responded with emotion. "That was a beautiful explanation. Just think about the impact it would have if all the people who are complaining that we've taken God out of our schools would encourage their children to take God to school in their hearts everyday and show his love to others in, as Mark said, the laboratory - a place to put learning to the test."

Susan observed, "Mr. Chairman, I appreciate your allowing us to have this discussion that we've had tonight. I have found it enlightening. Honestly, I have completely changed my position on the issue after hearing this discussion. I may be wrong but I believe that many citizens in our community are in the same boat that I was in and they would benefit from hearing this discussion."

"I move that our board instruct our superintendent to immediately begin the process of making our school system neutral on matters of religion and further, that we instruct him to bring back to the board at our next meeting recommended policies that would cause our system to be in compliance with religious neutrality. I am confident that this board wants to focus on our assigned task of providing a quality public education to our students and avoid having our school district to become a battlefield for wars rooted in religion."

Sylvia quickly seconded the motion.

Don preceded his vote with the statement, "I've listened carefully to the arguments that have been made tonight leading up to this motion. I understand what you have said and I see that I need to think long and hard about my position on these issues. One thing for certain, I do not want to waste the financial resources of our school district in a legal battle, but I'm still a long way from being able to vote for this motion."

The motion carried 5-2 with both Ron and Don voting against it.

Following the vote, Michael once again reminded the board of its pledge to help the community be informed on school issues and board positions. He called for reflective comments from any board member and asked for ideas about what the board might do to help the community be informed on this issue.

Mark expressed appreciation that education reporter Margie McBee was present at the meeting. He thanked her for her objective and straightforward reporting and observed that the fastest way to get information to the public was through her coverage of the meeting.

Sylvia suggested that the Presidents of all PTA/PTO's in the county be invited to an informational meeting with Lindell and Michael to discuss the board's position and to seek their help in getting the message to the community.

Susan added a suggestion that the presidents be encouraged to invite a representative of the board to speak at the next meeting at their school.

Michael asked Mark if he would be willing to write an op-ed piece for the local newspaper. He said that Mark had made some points that needed to be shared with the community. Mark agreed to do so.

Mark's Reflection

When Mark reached home, he told Maggie that he was extremely proud of the board. "I never thought I'd see the day that this board would be able to deal with such an emotional issue in such a logical and responsible manner. I have the deepest respect for the members of our board. Sylvia's strong stand which was not of her personal preference as a Christian was very effective." He thought that if the correct decision could be made without challenging Don's statement about America as a Christian nation, it was best not to challenge it. He thought that this was another demonstration that even when members disagree with the majority of the board, they serve a useful function.

He felt the board was fortunate to have Margie McBee as education reporter. He thought her report would be fair and helpful with community understanding of this issue. He was pleased to have the responsibility of writing an op-ed to help the community better understand the issue.

Questions for Discussion

1. What did you like or dislike about how the Progress County Board handled this issue?
2. To what extent is a local board of education required to have no policy or permit no procedure that promotes the establishment of religion or prohibits the free exercise thereof?
3. Both Ron and Don voted against the motion to make the school system free of religion. How do you think they feel about the board's decision? Were they listened to and treated with respect?
4. How important is it to respect all religions in the schools by endorsing or promoting none?
5. How would you react to the practice of promoting a religion that was very different from yours?

CHAPTER 23

To Pray Or Not To Pray, That Is The Question

MANY PEOPLE IN the community were excited that the high school band had been invited to participate in the Orange bowl parade and related activities. The band director submitted a request, approved by the principal to the school board for permission to go to Orlando for four days and also to raise money to provide funds necessary to make the trip. (Board permission was required by policy for out-of-state trips lasting longer than one night. All other field trips could be approved by the Superintendent.)

Subsequent to the board's approval of both requests, a local automobile dealer who wanted to help the band raise money, offered to pay $1500 for a sponsored band performance in a special event to honor veterans. The band members were delighted to receive the invitation and voted unanimously to participate in the event.

The band's performance with outstanding and the $1500 was a significant boost to the fund-raising effort. Unfortunately, when board members, the superintendent and the principal each received calls from the mother of a 15 year old girl who was a student at the school. Her calls were not made for the purpose of complimenting the performance of the band. She strenuously objected to the fact that public prayer was a part of the program in which the high school band had participated. A mother who described herself as a Wiccan, requested that she be included on the agenda to air her complaint at the next board meeting.

Lindell and Michael, meeting as the executive committee, discussed how to handle her request. Her daughter was not a member of the band. They decided it would be a good idea to let her appear before the board and use her appearance to help clarify this issue for both the members of the board and the community.

Each second-guessed their decision when she appeared before the board. She was aggressive and hostile. She took no time to make pleasantries. She described the incident and lambasted the band director and principal for allowing students to participate.

"This was a flagrant violation of the law," Alice Anderson told the board. "Our public schools are for all children, whether Catholic, Baptist, Quaker, atheist, Buddhist, Jewish or agnostic. The schools are supported by all taxpayers and therefore should be free of religious observances and coercion." She continued by asking that the principal and the band director both be disciplined for their severe lack of judgment and she suggested that the board modify its policy to prohibit appearances of the band and other student groups at events where they would be subjected to religious activity.

The board patiently listened until her three minutes were exhausted.

In spite of her total lack of charm, Michael politely thanked her for her appearance and asked, "Just for clarification, is your daughter a member of the band or was she for some other reason required by the school to be present at this event?"

"She was there as an observer. She is a student in the school and has friends in the band. She wanted to hear them play," Mrs. Anderson responded. "She was not required to be there but she should not have to sacrifice hearing her friends play in order to avoid being subjected to an illegal activity. There should be no religious activity in any program in which students are required to participate. That is clearly what is meant by separation of church and state."

"Could she have listened to the band play and have left immediately afterward?" Don asked.

"Certainly she could have but that would have been rude and should not be necessary," she replied. "I have made a great effort to teach my daughter not to be rude," she continued.

Michael thanked her again for sharing her concerns with the board. He suggested that the board might want to discuss this matter further at its next meeting. He asked if the board would find it helpful to have the school board attorney prepare a legal brief on the issue or if the board would like to hear from anyone else regarding the issue.

Ron said he didn't need to hear from anyone else regarding the incident but he would like for the board to broaden the issue to have a discussion about putting prayer back into the schools. He declared that one of his goals when he ran for a seat on the school board was putting public prayer back in the schools and that he had no doubt that a majority of the citizens who lived in the school district favored putting public prayer back in the schools. He said that it was a frequent topic of conversation at his church and he speculated that it would have unanimous support among the members of his church.

Susan said that the issue of prayer in the schools was raised a number of times during her campaign for election to the board. She said that she suspected that Ron was right about the majority of the community favoring putting prayer back in the schools. She admitted that she did not know all that a school board member should know about the issue. She said it would be helpful to her if all board members could receive a legal memorandum from the school board attorney regarding the issue. She said that she thought it would be helpful for the board to have at least limited discussion of the issue at the next board meeting.

Mark suggested that the executive committee select one pro speaker and one con speaker on the issue at the next meeting. He suggested that each speaker be given five minutes to summarize the pro and con arguments related to public prayer in the schools. He said this would allow the board to have a more informed discussion on the issue after hearing the speakers.

Don reminded the board that it needed to resolve the issue brought before it tonight by Mrs. Anderson. He said he didn't think it was necessary for the board to always respond to "certain members of our community who seem to thrive on being perpetually offended." He said that he personally did not think there was an issue but he would like for the school board attorney to include the issue raised by Mrs. Anderson in his legal opinion so that the board could put that issue to rest before it began the broader discussion of prayer in schools.

Michael brought the discussion to a close by summarizing, "If it is agreeable to all board members, we will instruct Lindell to request an opinion from the school board attorney on the legality of the is-sue brought before us tonight. After considering the legal opinion, the board will take action on the issue brought before us tonight if it deems action to be prudent. And, the Executive Committee will in-vite a speaker for and against public prayer in schools. We will allow each five minutes to summarize the arguments and we will follow those presentations with a discussion limited to 30 minutes on pub-lic prayer in schools. Then the board may determine that no action is needed but, at the least, the presentations and the discussion will be instructive to both the board and the community. Board members nodded their heads in agreement.

Susan said, "Mr. Chairman, I so move." Sylvia seconded the motion and the board approved unanimously.

"Mr. Chairman," Mark said, "I just want to say that I feel much better about asking our attorney to spend his time preparing to share information directly on a legal issue before the board rather than paying him to sit here listening to our discussions and feeling that he should be able to render an opinion on the spot with no time for research. I commend the board for its wisdom in that decision."

The next board packet contained a legal memorandum from Bob Lawson, the school board attorney, citing several cases and concluding that neither school board policy nor the law was broken when the high school band played at an event that began and ended with a prayer. The opinion said that because the event occurred on private property, was organized by a private group, did not involve direct action of any school employee, and was not a required activity for students because all members of the band had voted unanimously to participate — it violated neither the law nor school board policy.

The board packet also included a concise legal summary on the issue of school prayer that board attorney Lawson had prepared.

At the next school board meeting, Lindell summarized the memorandum at Michael's request. Then, Michael asked if any board member had questions or other comments. When there were none, he concluded that the board needed to take no action on the issue. No member of the board objected.

Michael reminded the board that it had requested the executive committee to find two speakers on the issue of public prayer in schools-one for and one against.

He introduced the pro speaker, Rev. Alex Milhouse pastor of Cornerstone Church. He thanked Rev. Milhouse for coming and informed him that a tone would sound at the end of five minutes and that he should finish the sentence if he were making one at the chime and conclude his remarks at that time.

Pastor Milhouse lavished the board with praise for considering what he judged to be an extremely important issue, one he called the "key to the success of the public schools" He thanked the board for choosing him to make a presentation. He spoke with enthusiastic fervor for five minutes and made the following points.

- To ban school prayer diminishes the religious freedom of students who want to pray and forces them to act according to the dictates of a non-religious minority.
- A simple and voluntary school prayer does not amount to the government establishing a religion.
- School prayer would address the needs of the whole person. Schools must do more than train children's minds academically. They must also nurture their souls and reinforce the values taught at home and in the community.
- School prayer would result in many societal benefits. Since the Supreme Court banned school prayer in 1963:
- Murder rate tripled;
- Violent crime went up 544%;
- Divorce rate more than doubled;
- Children living in fatherless households increased from 6% to 40%.
- The public school system has tragically disintegrated as evidenced by the rise in school shootings, increasing drug use, alcoholism, teen pregnancy, and HIV transmission.

He concluded that school prayer can help combat each of these issues, instill a sense of morality and is desperately needed to protect our children.

Michael thanked Pastor Milhouse for his enthusiastic presentation. Then, he introduced Dr. Henry Fox from the First Amendment Center at Vanderbilt University to present the case against public prayer in public schools. Dr. Fox emphasized that his comments were all about public school sponsored prayer, not student-initiated, voluntary prayer. He read his speech to the board and finished just before the dong sounded to signal that his five minutes were up. He made the following points.

- Prayer is private, and schools are public. Even Jesus spoke against school prayer in Matthew 6:5-6 when He said, "Thou shalt not be as the hypocrites are: for they love to pray standing in the synagogues and in the corners of the streets, that they may be seen of men..."But thou, when thou prayest, enter into thy closet, and when thou hast shut thy door, pray to thy Father which is in secret." (KJV)
- School sponsored prayer violates the Establishment Clause of the First Amendment which provides that the government shall make no law respecting the establishment of religion. Because public schools are government funded, prayer led by school officials or incorporated into the school routine amounts to government-established religion.
- Public schools are intended for education, not religious observance or proselytization.
- Prayer in school is already legal. Students are already allowed to pray on a voluntary basis (in a non-disruptive way) so formal school prayer is unnecessary.
- School prayer may lead to intolerance. Students who abstain from participation in school prayer have frequently been ostracized.

- School prayer is inherently coercive and cannot be implemented in a way that is truly voluntary.
- The public school system was created for all students and is supported by all taxpayers. It should remain neutral on religious issues over which students and taxpayers will differ.
- Since no formal school prayer could honor the tenets of all the religions and their various denominations practiced in the U.S., prayer should be reserved for the home, religious institutions and private gatherings of the individual student's choice.
- School prayer usurps the role of parents and religious institutions who desire to provide instruction in keeping with their own beliefs.

Michael thanked Dr. Fox for his presentation and the time that he had spent in preparing it.

Michael reminded Ron that he had requested that this discussion be included on the agenda and asked if he had a proposal for the board.

Ron said that he appreciated the presentations made by Dr. Fox and Rev. Milhouse. However, he said that he thought that Rev. Milhouse's presentation made a compelling argument that the board should seriously consider adopting a policy to allow public prayer in the schools.

"Who do you want to do the praying?" Mark asked.

"The principal or the teachers or the students." Ron answered. "Anyone who wants to. I'm not in favor of making them pray."

"What if the principal or teacher happens to be a member of a religion or even a denomination that differs considerably from yours?" asked Susan.

Jerry had been listening intently to the conversation but he now chipped in, "It seems like whatever religion most of the people in the community are a part of would dictate what prayers are said in the schools."

"I could not disagree more," said Sylvia. "If schools require students to say the prayers of the majority religion in each community, a lot of protestant kids will be reciting Catholic prayers because the Roman Catholic Church is the single largest denomination in our country. Would any of us favor sending protestant minorities into the hall while those left pray to the Virgin Mary? In a few school districts, Muslims outnumber other religions. Would we favor telling Christian students to cover their ears or go into the hall while the principal prays to Allah over the intercom? I don't think there is one of us who would want our children treated that way and we can't justify treating children of other religions that way."

"I probably shouldn't say this," Sylvia continued, "but I wonder how many of those clamoring most for prayer in our schools use any of the sixteen hours a day when their children aren't in school to pray with them? I know for certain that some people who have encouraged me to support prayer in our schools don't even take their children to church on the weekend."

In an effort to keep the discussion moving toward a conclusion, Michael asked, "As we conclude our discussion, is there a motion on Ron's proposal?"

"I don't believe that any action is needed," Mark said. "What I heard Ron saying was that he wanted to ensure that prayer is permitted in our schools--not required. That's already the case." He continued by reading from Bob Lawson, the school board attorney's legal memorandum, "Students have a right to pray alone or gather in groups to pray as long as they are not disruptive to the school environment. The law in our country prohibits us from preventing students from praying when it is not disruptive. Although schools may not promote religion, schools may not violate the free exercise of religion. That includes prayer in schools."

"Can't we require students to say the Lord's prayer or have a student pray over the school intercom every day?" Jerry asked.

"Bob's opinion says clearly that school officials are prohibited by the establishment clause from promoting religion," Mark responded. "Principals or teachers leading students in prayer is clearly promoting religion. Here is the situation in a nutshell. We can't require students to pray but we can't prohibit them from praying unless they are doing it in a disruptive manner."

"How could students pray in a disruptive manner?" Jerry asked.

Sylvia responded, "If they were praying when they are supposed to be doing something else it is disruptive. It's fine for students to gather before school or during lunch to pray but if they cut classes because they are having a prayer meeting, that is disruptive."

Michael asked Lindell if he had a recommendation or a comment. Lindell said he thought the board had covered the subject well and said that he agreed that no action was needed. He said that it appeared to him that the board had exactly what it wanted: the opportunity for those who want to pray but no requirement that anyone must pray or participate in a prayer service.

Michael expressed appreciation to the members of the board for the quality of discussion. He suggested that unless a member of the board wanted to make a motion on the subject, he would move on to the next item on the agenda. Interestingly, no one made a motion.

Mark's Reflection

On the way home, Mark reflected on the discussion about prayer in the schools. He agreed with Michael that the quality of the discussion was excellent. He also thought that the discussion would be viewed favorably by the community because everyone present saw the board deliberating on a controversial subject in a responsible manner. Some members of the board had some very strong feelings on either side of the issue but they were reasonable during a discussion and listened well to opposing viewpoints. "We're continuously becoming a better board." Mark said to himself. "Our board is making a difference in our school system and I believe that our community is recognizing and appreciating our approach to handling issues."

Michael's spirits were lifted even more when he read the article written by education reporter, Margie McBee about the board's discussion. He recalled that the board had identified one of its responsibilities was to help the community understand educational issues and the board's position on them. He was so favorably impressed with the accuracy, completeness and fairness of the article that he picked up the phone to call and thank Margie for her excellent work

Questions for Discussion

1. **What percent of the people in your community feel that prayer has been excluded from schools? Why do they feel this way?**
2. **How would parents who want prayer put back in the schools feel about requiring teachers of faiths radically different than their own to lead their child's class in prayer each morning?**
3. **How consistent is this decision of the board with its commitment to serve all the children of all the people?**
4. **What do you like or dislike about how the board handled this issue?**
5. **How would you evaluate the board's use of its attorney in this case?**

CHAPTER 24

Changing The School Culture

MARK BUMPED INTO Sally Bush at the grocery store on Saturday. She was wearing a bright red athletic suit with a T-shirt that read, "Some people believe in imaginary friends. I believe in imaginary numbers."

Sally had been a middle school math teacher for nineteen years. He asked her how things were going at school and she seemed to be more than happy to give him a full report.
"I'm thrilled with the progress my students are making," she said. I can see significant improvement in the knowledge and skills our students are bringing from elementary school. Apparently, our elementary teachers are doing a much better job of teaching math these days. At least, the students that I have in my class are better prepared. On the other hand, I've never had students who are less appreciative of what teachers and other school staff members do for them each day. It doesn't seem to occur to them to even say "Thank You" to people who go above and beyond the call of duty to help them."

"Are you saying that is a new phenomenon?" Mark asked.

"I think it's getting worse each year," Sally responded. "Rachel Peterson, our music teacher, worked so hard planning and preparing for a special music production with the eighth-graders. She said that she had her doubts about the success of the program after the first couple of practices but after they'd worked so hard, the presentation was nearly flawless. She could hardly believe the progress that the students made. While she was very pleased with the production, she was very disappointed that only one student expressed appreciation to her for the extra work that she had done in them to prepare for the program. She said that we were failing our students by not being intentional about helping to develop in them an attitude of gratitude."

"That's interesting," Mark said. "How do you feel about it?"

"I totally agree with her," Sally answered. "I've been concerned about this for sometime and I've had a number of other teachers and school staff members mention it to me. Don't you think that learning to recognize and express appreciation for what others do for you is an important lesson for our students?"

"I do," Mark said. "It has a great deal to do with students' ability to work well with others and it consequently impacts their ability to succeed."

"We're leaving a hole in our student's education if we don't help them learn to recognize what others do for them and express appreciation for it, Sally warned. "I heard that the school board is in the process of articulating a vision and is asking the community to suggest what we expect from our schools. I wish the board would discuss the importance of appreciation and maybe initiate the development of a plan for teaching appreciation to our students on a systemwide basis," Sally challenged Mark.

Mark hadn't spent much time thinking about the board's responsibility to help instill in students an attitude of gratitude. Sally's comment kept running through his mind. The more he considered it, the more important he thought it was for students to learn appreciation. If he wasn't totally convinced that it was the board's responsibility to initiate the development of a strategy for dealing with it on a systemwide basis, he thought that he must ask the board to consider the possibility.

On Monday, Mark called Lindell and asked him if he could spare 10 minutes in the next couple of days to discuss an issue with him. He told Lindell that there was no urgency. He just wanted to throw out an idea and get a reaction. Lindell said he was available that afternoon about 2 PM. They agreed to meet then.

Mark laid out the issue and asked Lindell if he thought it appropriate for the board's consideration. Lindell said it was an important issue and highly appropriate for the board's consideration. He said that one reason school boards were needed was to raise concerns about things that were not being done in the schools that should be done. He also said that he would give the issue some serious thought. He said that he had heard a presentation at AASA by a Tennessee's Superintendent, about an employee appreciation program they had implemented a couple of years ago. He remembered that she said it had changed the culture of their school system. He said he had been favorably impressed with the program and that he had intended to follow up on it but had not yet done so. He told Mark that he would follow up immediately and get back to him.

Two days later, Lindell called Mark to report that he had investigated the employee appreciation program in Anderson County as he promised to do. He said that he was highly impressed with the program and believed it held some real potential for our school system. He asked Mark to drop by and chat with him about it. Mark agreed to do so.

In his meeting with Mark, Lindell summarized what he had discovered about the program. Anderson County, as well as many other school districts in Tennessee, is participating in a program that was developed and made available through Utrust, an unemployment compensation trust for school boards in Tennessee. The program was originally established to boost the morale of employees and discourage them from leaving their jobs as school system employees. It was soon discovered that students learning to express appreciation was every bit as important as the impact it had on employees.

In fact, the program greatly improved relationships between staff and students. When students paid more attention to what school employees did for them each day and began to express appreciation to the employees, both student and employee respect for each other increased. As respect increased so did relationships and appreciation. Likewise, morale increased for both students and staff. When morale increased, so did performance of both students and staff increase. Then, attendance of both groups increased and suddenly the school became a better place to both work and learn.

The model, developed by Utrust, uses two student leadership teams. The first, called the A-Team (A for appreciation), plans and implements eight appreciation days during the school year. On each appreciation day, a different group of employees is individually recognized and appreciated. The Utrust model also uses a G–Force (G for gratitude) made up of student leaders from each homeroom or classroom to promote the expression of appreciation throughout the year.

Lindell concluded his summary by stating, "The program is extremely well-organized so there is no burden on faculty or staff. I am convinced that it is a superb way to teach our students to recognize and appreciate those who do things to make their lives better. It does not infringe on class time and it is fun for students and staff. I will introduce this program at our next principal's meeting and I'm confident that they will embrace it. If so, I'll recommend it to the board. If we can secure board approval, we can get this program rolling next year."

"I certainly appreciate your prompt attention to this matter," Mark said. "Seldom are we able to respond so rapidly to a request from some of our teachers. I suspect they'll be pleasantly surprised and we can see if they show an attitude of gratitude," Mark jested.

Lindell sent out information about the program in his weekly notes to board members. He urged members to go on the Utrust website (utrust.org) to see photos and videos, read success stories and find additional information about the program that he would recommend at the next meeting.

Following Lindell's recommendation at the board meeting, Michael asked for comments or questions from the board.

Sylvia responded, "I can't overemphasize how pleased I am with this recommendation from our superintendent. Just yesterday, I was read-ing an article by Dr. Oz which he concluded by saying, 'People who practice gratitude tend to be more creative, bounce back more quick-ly from adversity, have a stronger immune system and have stronger social relationships.' The article got me thinking that we needed to do something about helping our students to learn to better express grati-tude." Sylvia turned to Lindell and continued, "It's amazing that only one day later you bring this recommendation. I'm delighted to make a motion that we approve participation in this program."

"I second the motion," Don said. "I believe that this program will have a major positive impact on our students, our staff and our commu-nity. Students won't just be showing gratitude to school employees, they will be more likely to show appreciation for the things that their parents, their Sunday school teachers and their neighbors do and it will impact our entire community. The superintendent from Anderson County said that the program had changed the culture of their school district. I'm very hopeful that it will change the culture in ours."

After the board unanimously approved Lindell's recommendation and adopted the resolution to participate in the program, the audience applauded.

Mark's Reflection

As Mark drove home after the board meeting, he thought to himself," It's great to be able to see a suggestion brought to a board member become a proposal supported by the superintendent and adopted by the board become a reality so quickly. And, he thought, it makes it even better when the audience expresses appreciation for the outcome. I think we're becoming a better board and I feel certain that our community is recognizing it. This is one of the times when it's great to be a school board member."

Questions for Discussion

1. How important is it for a school board to express appreciation to employees for what they do?
2. Why is it important that appreciation be expressed to individuals rather than to a group of employees?
3. How would each of the following be improved as a result of employees continuously receiving expressions of genuine appreciation: morale, attendance, performance, relationships?
4. Would you like for your children to attend a school where they are taught to be grateful and to express that gratitude to others? Why or why not?
5. In what ways do expressions of appreciation and gratitude contribute to creating a healthy workplace?

CHAPTER 25

Making Students More Safe At School

JERRY SAID THAT ever since the shooting at the Sandy Hook Elementary School he had been asked over and over again how the school board planned to deal with student safety. "I have no idea what we plan to do," he said. "What am I supposed to tell people the board intends to do about student safety? I would like to be able to assure our community that the children attending our schools will be safe."

Michael responded, "We need to have this discussion in an open school board meeting. It's a big issue and the community needs to know that it has our attention. In fact, the issue is bigger than this board. Most anything significant that we do will require additional funds which the board does not have. This session today is about what we're already doing, how we do it and why we do it. May we please hold the safety discussion until a regular school board meeting?"

Everyone agreed that would be more appropriate and Michael promised to put the item on the board's annual agenda for a discussion three weeks later.

The subject of school safety on the school board agenda drew a crowd of more than 200 to the regular meeting of the Progress County School Board. Michael introduced the topic by announcing that it was not the intent of the board to solve this issue tonight but to begin the discussion, hear suggestions from the community and perhaps formulate a plan. He invited persons in the audience to raise their hand and be recognized any time they wanted to offer a comment relevant to the board's discussion. He urged them to keep responses short and to the point and he advised that board members would receive priority recognition and that, depending on the number who wished to speak, all citizens may not get to speak tonight. He said that if they did not get to make their comments public tonight they should submit them in writing to the superintendent in the next few days.

Michael asked if Superintendent Lindell Sharp would like to begin the discussion.

"We know that student safety is our highest priority," said Superintendent Sharp. "When parents drop off their children in the morning they are trusting us with a huge responsibility. We accept that responsibility as if they're our own children. It's our highest priority that children feel safe and are safe. However," Lindell warned, "We must be careful that we don't have a knee jerk reaction and take actions that will give the school-community a false sense of security that will come back to bite us. Let's don't jump too quickly and create an oversimplified response to a complex issue."

"You make a great point," said Susan. "I know very little about school safety but I know that I do not want our board to panic and make our schools look like prisons. Let's examine the issue in a thoughtful manner and make decisions that are rational and effective. We need to be certain that we don't waste a lot of money that could much be better spent on enhancing learning."

"I don't think it would be wasting money to install safety glass in each of our schools and build chain link fences around them to keep dangerous people out," Jerry replied. "That's not a complicated process and we could begin it immediately."

"Jerry, that might be simple but we don't have the money to do it," Susan responded. "Even if we had the money, think about this. We've never had a single problem with firearms or any other major safety issue in the history of Progress County Schools. I don't think that we need to install safety glass or build chain link fences around our schools just because some other school boards are doing it. I've never heard of a school shooter breaking a glass to get inside the school. I think that would be a knee jerk reaction - exactly what Lindell described a minute ago."

"I agree with Susan," Sylvia volunteered. "Installing safety glass in schools seems far fetched and I hate to even think about building ugly chain link fences around our schools. What kind of message does that send to our children?"

"It sends a message that we care about them and we're willing to take whatever steps are necessary to protect them," Jerry said.

"It seems to me that a person committed to violence at a school could simply lean an extension ladder against a chain link fence and be over it in a jiffy or they could shoot through the fence," Mark added. "Wouldn't a chain link fence be more effective in deterring vandalism rather than a shooter? Vandals are concerned with getting away after the vandalism. Most school shooters don't expect to escape."

A young lady who identified herself as Janice Williams, the mother of a second grade girl and a 4th grade boy said that she simply wanted the board and superintendent to guarantee the safety of her children at Lincoln Elementary (a school built for community access with eleven outside doors). She said, "I continuously warn both of my children to look behind every tree and watch for strangers. I tell them every day to keep an eye out for someone with a gun and to run if they see one." She added, "I'm scared to death for their safety and now they're almost too scared to come to school. I just want them to be safe."

Dr. Wilford Sampson, a well known and respected psychologist and community resident, raised his hand to speak. After Michael recognized him, he said, "I think it is extremely important that schools are attractive and pleasant places as well as safe ones." He continued, "We learn from our surroundings; education may be caught as much as taught. There is no doubt that excessive measures to constrain potential violators, such as building chain link fences around schools, carry a heavy cost to our students."

He turned toward the previous speaker and said, "Mrs. Williams, I totally understand your concern for the safety of your children. However, I can assure you that excessive warnings to students about the potential dangers of attending schools do more harm than good and can directly be the cause of a child becoming a 'victim' in terms of emotional/ mental expectations. Balancing reasonable safety measures with provisions to allow children to be children continues to challenge our wisdom." Then he turned toward the board and said. "We are fortunate that our community has elected competent and caring people to serve on our school board. I applaud you for having a discussion of this sort tonight and for considering differing points of view."

"This discussion has caused me to change my mind." Ron confessed. "I originally thought that we should build fences around the schools and do it quickly. After hearing this discussion, I think it would be a major waste of money. Even if we have vandalism in one of our schools, which fortunately, I have never heard of us having, chances are it would cost far less to repair the damage than it would cost to install chain link fences."

Don offered an observation and suggestion: "I don't think we have anyone on the board who knows much about school safety. I think we should have the district undergo a safety evaluation by an independent safety expert"

A man in the audience vigorously waved his hand to speak. Michael recognized him and the man identified himself as Harley Brooks, father of four children who attended Progress County Schools. He said the greatest safety need was to have safety drills.

"How many kids in the United States have died in school fires in the last 50 years?" he asked. "Zero," he responded, answering his own question. "How many kids in the U.S. have died in active shooter situations in the last 50 years?" he asked. "Hundreds." He again answered himself. "The difference is that our schools hold monthly fire drills. This board should implement mandatory monthly intruder drills if you want to do the thing that will make the most difference to the safety of our children," he concluded.

"Not a bad idea," Don said before Michael had time to thank Mr. Brooks for his comment. "If we had SROs in all of our schools, they could be in charge of the training that needs to occur in all classes and they could be responsible for conducting the drills."

"I like the idea of expanding the number of SROs and having them in charge of safety training and drills," Ron added. "But, I'd really like to see the staff explore the possibility of having the sheriff's office train some of our current employees to add SRO responsibilities to their current duties. For example, we might have some bus drivers who would love to add some hours to their work day and stay at school as SROs. Or there might be a custodian who would welcome the opportunity to take SRO training and add safety duties to his or her current responsibilities." As an afterthought, Ron said, " The more people we have in a school with that kind of training and responsibilities, the safer our schools will be."

Jerry endorsed Ron's idea. "I think Ron has offered a creative way to get more SROs into the schools. I had not thought of using current employees in an expanded role but I like the idea. We might also even consider volunteers who would undergo the training and donate a few hours each week as a volunteer SRO."

Sylvia cautioned, "I'm not trying to pour cold water on the idea of having adult volunteers help provide safety services. I think the idea is certainly worth further thought, but I have serious reservations about increasing the number of law enforcement officials in our schools. There are credible studies now showing that there may be more negatives than positives resulting from SROs in schools. I just want us to consider this research and look creatively at the issue. We might develop a better model."

Sheriff Mike Jones who was in the audience stood to be recognized and said that he was fascinated by Ron's idea and that he thought it had merit. He said that he was not pushing for more resource officers because he, frankly, was not persuaded that assigning an SRO to each school was the best use of the county's resources. He said that training current employees for additional safety responsibilities might work well if they were carefully selected. He said that Jerry's idea of volunteer safety officers in the schools did not strike him negatively and he offered to conduct the training if the board chose to go either route. He said that he might know a few people who would be excellent volunteer safety officers but he'd like to explore both ideas with Lindell and join him in further evaluating the proposals.

Michael thanked Sheriff Jones and said that the session was even more productive than he had imagined.

Mark agreed that the session was productive and meaningful. Then he observed, "We want our community to recognize that the board and staff of Progress County Schools recognize that school safety is a major priority in the operation of our public schools. If we stopped the practice of bringing large groups of students together for "education," we could greatly reduce or even eliminate the risk of mass tragedy but what would we lose by doing so? Would that action be a good one for our society?"

Mark continued, "This school board and our staff, no matter what kind of weapons we may employ, can never guarantee parents such as Mrs. Williams that their children will be totally safe from harm when they come to school. Some deranged person could set up outside the school and ambush students and their parents as they leave school or even ambush a school bus loaded with students. Even though we can not assure them absolute safety, we can assure them that we have taken and will continue taking all reasonable actions to protect children and adults at school."

Michael could tell that several board members had questions or comments in response to Mark's comments but he thought the purpose of the discussion had been achieved and that the discussion had gone on long enough for one evening so he again thanked all persons who participated in the discussion both for their presence and for their participation. Then, he asked Superintendent Sharp for his recommendation about how to proceed.

Lindell pointed out that every school in Progress County has "sound safety measures" in place. He said that his cabinet and all principals recently had a session on evaluating safety measures and that they have generated some ideas to make campuses even safer and plan to move forward with those recommendations. He said that each school holds periodic lock down drills, fire drills and "duck, cover, hold" drills to prepare schools for emergencies. He said that he would like for the board and the community to share with him, his cabinet members or any school principal any suggestions regarding the improvement of safety in the school district.

He recommended that the board allow three months for them to complete their study and their development of a proposed total school system safety plan. He promised to report back with the plan and recommendations that might include a request for additional funding to implement the plan.

Sylvia moved that the board accept Superintendent Sharp's recommendation and that the board schedule a report on its annual agenda for three months hence. Don seconded the motion and Michael called for discussion on the motion.

Susan said, "I'm very much in favor of the motion and I do not want to throw a monkey wrench into it, but before we vote, I am deeply concerned that bullying and harassment has led to dangerous situations for students." This is a safety issue for all students, especially lesbian, gay, bisexual or transgender (LGBT) students, as well as students perceived to be LGBT." She said that she was not seeking to amend the motion but was simply asking the administration to please give some consideration to this issue in their deliberations.

The board voted unanimously to adopt the motion.

Mark's reflection

Mark's reflection of the meeting focused mostly on the safety discussion. He was very pleased with the level of discussion and interaction among board members and their reliance on Lindell and his staff to deal with the board's concerns. He felt that the board had shared the issue with the community and had given the public an opportunity to help find a solution to the problem. In his opinion, the board had done exactly what it should do and instead of trying to take on the administration's responsibilities, had stopped at about the right point to leave the details with the superintendent and his staff. He was also pleased that the Sheriff was supportive and willing to be involved. He hoped that the board would continuously use the resources of the community and build support and cooperation for the schools. He smiled as he concluded that the board had done a respectable job of exercising community leadership tonight.

Mark thought back to the day he decided to run for a seat on the school board. He remembered his hope that he could make a difference and help the board become an effective board. He thought back to the issues the board had faced since his election and he smiled as he concluded our board has come together and while we disagree about many issues we, for the most part, have learned to disagree agreeably. And, he mused, "Our board has earned the respect of our community. We've made great progress in viewing our differences of opinion as aiding rather than hindering decision-making that represents and is generally accepted by our diverse community." He believed that the board was even creating public opinion rather than reacting to it.

Mark was pleased that he had accepted the challenge of running for a seat on the school board. He had made the right decision in nominating Michael for school board president. He didn't want to be self aggrandizing but he could not help but think that the Progress County School Board had made enormous progress and he took great satisfaction that he was accomplishing what he had hoped to do.

Questions for Discussion

1. **What questions should a board ask when determining whether or not to approve a recommended safety device or procedure?**
2. **Can you think of an instance where a school board bought a safety device or implemented a procedure that did more harm than good?**
3. **Why do you connect increased safety with law enforcement? Are there other approaches to accomplish the same purpose?**

4. How should a school board go about determining whether to have SRO's in all of its schools?
5. How should the board engage the community in deciding what safety measures to implement in the schools?

CHAPTER 26

Assessing Progress
In Progress County

BEFORE THE END of the previous school board meeting, Michael reminded the board that according to its policy a formal self-evaluation was to occur in January. However, he suggested since Lindell would officially retire at the end of the month, he would like for the board to meet with him for an hour or so to informally assess the progress of the board and solicit Lindell's observations and recommendations for the board. He asked for and received unanimous approval of the board for an informal meeting with no agenda except reflections and assessing progress in board operations. The meeting would be open to the public but no minutes would be kept. Michael encouraged Lindell to reflect on board operations over the past year and be prepared to share his observations at the meeting. He encouraged board members to continue to do some self-reflection.

The meeting took place in a conference room at the school board offices so members could sit around the large conference table facing each other rather than at the more formal boardroom where members sat in a semi circle facing the audience. In addition to all board members and Lindell, Margie McBee and five school administrators were there. Michael had arranged for refreshments including finger sandwiches to be available.

Michael began the meeting by sharing a number of thoughtful, appreciative comments that he had prepared about Lindell and his service to the students, staff, community and schools of Progress County. Then, he invited Lindell to share his honest, forthright observations about working with the board during the past year.

Lindell began by thanking board members for their individual and collective support in providing him with what he called, "the strongest year of board support in his career." He commended the board for the way it had handled disagreements, complaints and compliments. He said that the number of community members sharing with him compliments about the board had steadily increased throughout the year. Then, he shared with the board, a list of observations and reflections that he had made. After reading it, he elaborated on each item on the list:

1. You have each shown a commitment to being a better board and becoming an effective member of the board.
2. You have improved in your ability to disagree agreeably and are continuing to become more skillful in that regard.
3. You have recognized that differences of opinion can be a strength rather than a weakness. We have a diverse community and the better the board understands the diversity of community thought, the better it will be able to reach wise decisions.
4. You have shown increased understanding and commitment to keep your focus on proper school board roles.
5. You have shown an increasing understanding, respect for and support of administrative roles and responsibilities.
6. You have explored the possibility and are working to become a more cohesive board that will be able to work through strong differences to lead in a single direction.

7. You are working toward listening to each other and showing respect for the opinions of others, including those with which you disagree.
8. Your dedication to community leadership has begun to produce the kind of results you had hoped for and will continue to do so as you hone those skills.
9. You have shown that you are able to create public opinion rather than simply reacting to it and it has paid off in increased community support for our public schools.
10. You have grown as a board in your acceptance of the role of the press. You have welcomed our education reporter and have been responsible and honest in your dealings with her. Our school system has nothing to hide and you have shown that you understand that.
11. You have grown in your understanding that school board meetings are one of our community's largest windows to the operation of our school district. Your conduct and focus during your meetings has been moving toward exemplary.
12. I have seen evidence that some members of the board feel responsibility to help each other become effective. That's important because a board can never achieve maximum effectiveness until every member is effective.

He concluded his remarks by again expressing his appreciation for the progress that the board had made during the last year. He said that he had high expectations of the board and that if he had worked with a board like this throughout his career, he would have had far fewer gray hairs and sleepless nights. He urged the board to continue its dedication to excellence and its commitment to lead the community in making schools the best places to work and learn.

Mark's Reflection

Mark considered Lindell's comments as documentation of what he had already concluded. He was proud of the Progress County Board of Education. He had not overlooked the fact that each of Lindell's observations was open-ended in the sense that he had not concluded that their mission was accomplished. Rather, he had implied that there was still progress to be made. Mark appreciated Lindell's recognition of board growth as well as his implied challenge to keep growing as a board and as individual board members. The evidence convinced him that the Progress County School Board has potential for greatness when its members are all aboard.

Questions for Discussion

1. What are the pros and cons of asking the superintendent to evaluate the performance of the board? Why would this practice be more likely to work if the superintendent is retiring or leaving?
2. What recommendations would you offer a board with regard to self-evaluation?
3. What are the pros and cons of using an outside facilitator?
4. What benefit are checklist evaluation forms as a tool to help a board to do self evaluation?
5. Identify three strengths and three weaknesses of the Progress County Board?

CHAPTER 27

Dealing With The Pandemic

A SPECIAL SESSION of the progress County Board of Education was called to deal with pandemic- related matters. After the meeting was called to order and formalities were handled, Michael asked Lindell to give the board an overview of the issues facing the school district.

Lindell and his staff gave a summary of the situation. He admitted that there was much that he and his staff didn't know. He said that the issues the school system is facing with regard to the pandemic is the greatest challenge of his career. He said the options for the opening of school in the fall that he and his staff have been studying will require new uses of time and space to ensure safety for students and staff. He warned that this was an urgent and immediate need that would require the board to make a number of decisions in a short time period.

Lindell informed the board that the school district had never faced a crisis to the extent of the present one. Then, he started to reel off what he said was "a few of the issues the board and staff would be forced to address." He said that, "Chief among the issues to be addressed was whether to start school on site and if so, how and when?"

Don interrupted," I know that's a complicated decision and I'm eager to hear the options that you're planning to share with us. I want to share with you before you go any further that my constituents are overwhelmingly in favor of resuming school full-time on site."

"That's not consistent with what I've been hearing in my district," Susan replied. "there are at least as many parents who have contacted me who do not want schools to open in person right now as there are who want school to begin on site. There's not an overwhelming response either way."

Ron suggested, "Childcare is an enormous problem for many people in our community. Parents have traditionally relied on schools to keep their children safe and engaged learning while they work."

Jerry agreed that, "Without question, many parents depend on schools for childcare."

Don said that his major concern was that he didn't want students to fall behind in their learning.

Susan said, "Whatever solution we finally adopt, we simply must include an option that does not require all students to return to school. We can not expect parents to send their children to school when they feel that it is unsafe to do so."

Mark acknowledged that people depended on the schools for childcare and said, "All of us prefer that students be full time learners at school when that is possible but it may very well be impossible without excessive risk. We are likely to find ourselves dealing with options and possibilities rather than the 'certainties' with which we are more comfortable."

Michael said that he had recently read that a motto emerging from the Great Flu Epidemic of 1918 was 'Education is important, but life and health are more important.' Perhaps, reminding the community that we agree, will help to allay fear that we will allow something bad to happen to their children." Then, he asked Lindell to continue with his briefing about the situation.

Lindell continued by listing some of issues that the staff is pursuing which included: how, and if, school can continue in days or weeks ahead; whether holding a double shift at some schools could accommodate the needs; whether on-line instruction is a practical alternative; whether students who depend on schools for food can be served if we go to virtual schooling; how state and federal funding will be affected; whether the state might grant a waiver for the annual number of school days or hours required; if testing requirements can be waived or modified; what to do about employees pay or unemployment for those who feel that it's unsafe to return; how teacher evaluation requirements will be affected; how data on student learning can be processed in ways to provide continuity and allow us to modify our approach."

Michael asked, "Is there anything that you'd like the board to do with regard to any of those items?

"Not now," Lindell replied, "I just wanted you to begin to think about all of the issues our staff is working on. We're facing an enormous challenge of building and creating new models of instruction. We know that it will require dual on-line and in-school platforms. We must have pervasive collaboration and it will demand creative thinking for design and implementation." Then, he put on the screen the following list of things the staff has discovered from its research:

- Major modifications may require staggered hours for students and teachers or alternate days or alternate weekly attendance by students.
- To avoid disruptions in continuity of learning the provision of digital devices, internet access and the utilization of digital

resources will be an absolute necessity.

- It may mean a major change in calendar, hours, alternating in-school and on-line instruction and use of staff resources will mean that principals and teachers will lead by being problem solvers and solution finders.
- What was once a choice of innovation or equity is now an absolute necessity to meet the needs of students and staff and provide a safe and secure environment.
- Preparing to open schools will necessitate the convention of class in school and class at home.
- Flexibility and adaptation in program and procedure will be essential.
- Expanded alliances at the district and school level will allow us to secure more good ideas and better equip us to handle new demands.

When Lindell paused, Jerry observed, "It's a good thing we designated our board as a learning community because I don't have the foggiest notion how to handle anything that you've mentioned. We have a lot of learning to do and I think that I am ready to get on with it."

"I totally agree, Mark said. "I'm grateful that we have a superintendent and staff who are up to the challenge. I appreciate their efforts in seeking assistance from those who have expertise in such matters. In the larger society we seem to be experiencing a crisis in credibility. Our board needs to be listening to Lindell and his staff and depending heavily on them to provide guidance and direction throughout this process. One of the things we ask of them is to help us to discern who and what to believe when faced with differing recommendations from experts."

Lindell promised the board that he and his staff would be extremely diligent in examining options as they develop plans to be recommended to the board. He urged the board to provide strong and

cohesive leadership during this crisis. He said it would have a tremendously positive impact on the community and its confidence
that the right things were being done regarding the education of its
children and youth. He urged the board members to share their best
thinking as the board made decisions during these trying times but to
be 100 percent supportive of whatever decisions the board makes for
the sake of unity and public support. He said the community would
look to the school board for leadership and warned that the leadership provided by the board and administration must be in a single
direction if we want maximum community confidence and support.

Michael said, "I'm confident that our board will rise to this challenge." The members began to nod their heads in agreement as if they
had reached consensus. Then, Michael turned to Lindell and asked,
"What's next?"

Lindell said, "Whatever course we choose, one thing is certain. We
no longer have an option about whether our students need digital
devices. Every student will need a digital device. We've chosen to
supplement our limited knowledge in this area by consulting with
one of our country's most knowledgeable experts, Dr. Mark Edwards.
We had earlier been reading some of his works- including three
most timely blogs written this summer to help school districts facing these tough decisions. His blogs are published on the site of
ReadWriteDigital- a company marketing data analysis tools. Dr.
Edwards was National School Superintendent of the Year for -among
other things his success in extending technology to every student in
his school district long before the pandemic. This approach was once
optional, now essential-once a choice, now a necessity.'

Greatly concerned about the cost of such an effort, Jerry inquired,
"Do you seriously consider that to be a possibility in Progress County?
Where will we ever find the money to do that?"

"Our staff raised that question with Dr. Edwards," Lindell said. "He said that districts all over the country have figured out how to do this by moving to digital content (replacing books, paper, and other expenses) and using on-line resources to save postage, print costs and numerous other costs and services. He suggested that we consider using a lease program that allows the cost of the devices to be paid for over 3-5 years. He gave us an impressive list of advantages for students that the digital devices provide. As we read and discussed the articles and blogs of Dr. Edwards, I noticed a couple of interesting things: our staff seemed to sense that a major change in our resources and our thinking will be necessary and yet, a strong sense of 'we can do it' was expressed."

As an afterthought, Lindell said, "Our staff is also exploring the possibility of receiving at least some federal funds from the CARES Act that is intended to cover costs associated with the pandemic. Additional resources from all levels of government may be required and provided."

Sylvia said, "I love the idea of every student having a digital device and I certainly agree with Dr. Edwards that numerous new possibilities become available to enhance learning. However, I suspect that we have a significant percentage of our students who don't have access to the internet. They can't do on-line learning without internet access."

Lindell replied, "Our staff is busy seeking ways to get internet access for all our students. We're working with Internet providers to find creative solutions. We're exploring the use of hot spots and mobile access design buses. We're also exploring the possibility of federal funds. We think our community will step us and help us meet this challenge."

"What are you thinking about the possibilities of getting our students back to on school site learning?" Don asked Lindell.

Lindell replied, "We know that social and physical distancing will be essential in any plan to bring students back into our schools, as will wearing masks. We're looking at various models to accommodate this including alternating days, weeks, split shifts during the day and even use of alternative facilities. We'll have a recommendation of what seems best for us. Our priority will be the safety of our students and staff. We very much do not want to open schools, even on a limited basis, and then have to close them."

As he prepared to adjourn the meeting, Michael thanked Lindell and his staff for the excellent work they are doing and expressed confidence in the forthcoming recommendations. "We recognize that your report did not include all that your staff is working on, but it does allow our meeting to provide a window into our system to help the community to know more about what is going on in their schools."

Lindell's attitude seemed unusually upbeat as he thanked Michael and the board for their continuing support. Then, he told them that they could expect the school staff to rise to the challenge. He surprised them by suggesting that after meeting the immediate challenge, the school district will be better because of changes forced by the pandemic. He said that providing digital devices for every student could significantly enhance instructional effectiveness by maximizing the use of digital resources and putting a greater emphasis on individualizing education for every student. He noted that unequal access to resources is, and has been, a major barrier to equity in learning. He said that he expected to see a bit of a shift from teaching to learning as students take on a greater role as collaborators in the learning process.

Mark's Reflection

Mark was highly impressed with the leadership Lindell was displaying in this pandemic crisis. He thought that Lindell seemed energized by what seemed to be an overwhelming challenge of dealing with the pandemic. He sincerely believed that Lindell was in the midst of what would be his most outstanding leadership achievement. He was grateful that Lindell had not abandoned ship since his retirement was imminent. He would encourage Lindell to extend his retirement date until at least the end of December.

As he thought back over the activities of the board in the previous year, he could not have been more pleased with the individual and collective progress. He concluded that the members were all aboard and that the board was on track and moving the school district toward what they envisioned it to become.

Questions for Discussion

1. **In Chapter 26, Lindell gave us a 12-point summary of the improvement made by the board. Which of these improvements served the board well as it faced an unprecedented challenge?**
2. **How will the reminder that "Education is important, but life and health are more important" be received in the community?**
3. **How did the discussion in this chapter provide a window to the community about a major issue of great concern?**
4. **Critique the board's interaction in this chapter. What could the board have done better in this chapter?**
5. **How will the community react to the possibility that the uniformity among schools will be altered by emerging differences within the attendance areas?**